WordPerfect ® 8

fast & easy

How to Order:

For information on quantity discounts contact the publisher: Prima Publishing, P.O. Box 1260BK, Rocklin, CA 95677-1260; (916) 632-4400. On your letterhead include information concerning the intended use of the books and the number of books you wish to purchase. For individual orders, turn to the back of this book for more information.

WordPerfect® 8

fast & easy

Diane Koers

PRIMA PUBLISHING

Publisher: Matthew H. Carleson
Managing Editor: Dan J. Foster
Acquisitions Editor: Jenny L. Watson
Development Editor: Kelli Crump
Project Editor: Kelli Crump
Copy Editor: Hilary Powers
Technical Reviewers: Dick Cravens, Ray Link
Interior Design and Layout: Marian Hartsough
Cover Design: Prima Design Team
Indexer: Katherine Stimson

ISBN: 0-7615-1083-4
Library of Congress Catalog Card Number: 97-65765
Printed in the United States of America

97 98 99 HH 10 9 8 7 6 5 4 3 2 1

To Vern

For always believing in me

Acknowledgments

I am deeply thankful to the many people at Prima Publishing who worked on this book. Thank you for all the time you gave and for your assistance.

To Jenny Watson for the opportunity to write this book and for her endless advice; to Debbie Abshier for introducing Jenny to me, and for always taking the time to talk with me and listen to my complaining; to Dick Cravens for helping make this book technically correct; and to Kelli Crump for all her assistance in the development of the book.

Lastly, to my husband. Thank you Vern, for all your support and neverending faith in me. Were all those carryout dinners and late nights worth it?

About the Author

Diane Koers owns and operates All Business Service, a software training and consulting business formed in 1988 that services the central Indiana area. In addition, she was a Certified Instructor for WordPerfect Corporation for many years. Diane, author of Prima's *Lotus 1-2-3 97 Visual Learning Guide* and a technical reviewer on many other books, also has experience developing and writing software training manuals for her clients' use.

Active in her church and civic activities, Diane enjoys spending her free time traveling and playing with her grandson and three Yorkshire Terriers.

Contents
at a Glance

PART III
WORKING WITH TABLES. 133

PART IV
USING MAIL MERGE 195

PART V
GETTING CREATIVE WITH GRAPHICS 231

PART VI
WORKING ON THE INTERNET 265

PART VII
APPENDIXES 305

Contents

PART II
FORMATTING A REPORT 63

PART V
GETTING CREATIVE WITH GRAPHICS 231

PART VI
WORKING ON THE INTERNET 265

Introduction

This new Visual Learning Guide from Prima Publishing will help you open up the power of Corel WordPerfect. WordPerfect is one of the leaders in word processing software. The product has been on the market for many years and has an outstanding reputation as being everything you could want in a word processor. Each time a new version of the software comes out, it has new features to use.

This book will show you how to accomplish the most common word processing tasks from writing a letter to creating a report to making a mass mailing. Visual Learning Guides teach you with a step-by-step approach, clear language, and color illustrations of exactly what you will see on your screen. The *WordPerfect 8 Visual Learning Guide* provides the tools you need to successfully tackle the potentially overwhelming challenge of learning to use WordPerfect 8. You will be able to quickly tap into the program's user-friendly design.

WHO SHOULD READ THIS BOOK?

The easy-to-follow, highly visual nature of this book makes it the perfect learning tool for a beginning computer user. However, it is also ideal for those who are new to this version of WordPerfect.

In addition, anyone using a software application always needs an occasional reminder about the steps required to perform a particular task. By using the *WordPerfect 8 Visual Learning Guide*, any level of user can look up steps for a task quickly without having to plow through pages of descriptions.

In short, this book can be used by the beginning-to-intermediate computer user as a learning tool or as a step-by-step task reference.

ADDED ADVICE TO MAKE YOU A PRO

You'll notice that this book uses steps and keeps explanations to a minimum to help you learn faster. Included in the book are a few elements that provide some additional comments to help you master the program, without encumbering your progress through the steps:

✦ **Tips** often offer shortcuts when performing an action, or a hint about a feature that might make your work in WordPerfect quicker and easier.

✦ **Notes** give you a bit of background or additional information about a feature, or advice about how to use the feature in your day-to-day activities.

In addition, helpful appendixes teach you WordPerfect tips and tricks and how to create an event calendar. When you finish, you can begin using the tips and calendar in your work right away!

Read and enjoy this Visual Learning Guide. It is certainly the fastest and easiest way to learn Corel WordPerfect 8. Enjoy!

Diane Koers

PART I
Creating the Perfect Document

1 Welcome to WordPerfect 8

Creating a document in WordPerfect involves a couple of steps. Since you will be at the Windows 95 desktop when you start, that's where we will begin in this book. In this chapter, you'll learn how to:

✦ **Start the WordPerfect program**

✦ **Enter text**

✦ **Enter a date**

✦ **Add special characters**

STARTING WORDPERFECT

Your screen may vary slightly from this figure if you have customized your Windows 95 desktop. You may also see some differences depending on whether you have installed the entire Corel WordPerfect Suite or just the WordPerfect program.

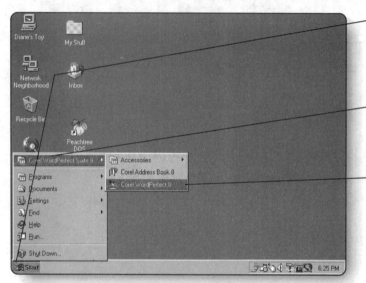

1. **Click** on the **Start button** in the lower left corner of your screen. The Start menu will appear.

2. **Click** on **Corel WordPerfect Suite 8**. A cascading menu will appear.

3. **Click** on **Corel WordPerfect 8**. A blank document will open.

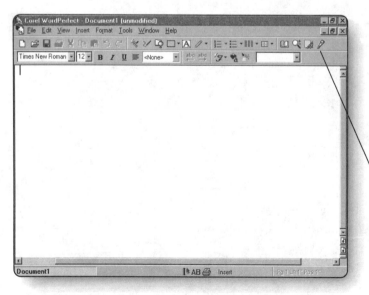

Many items you see when you open a new WordPerfect document are standard to any Windows 95 program. However, there are a few items that are specific to the WordPerfect program. These include the:

✦ **Toolbar**. A series of commonly used features of the WordPerfect program. These tools will remain the same no matter what feature of WordPerfect you are using.

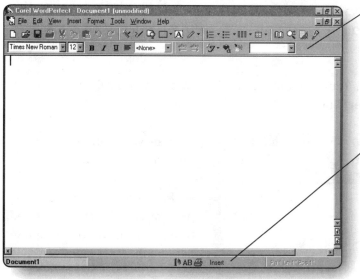

♦ **Property Bar**. A series of tools that will change according to the feature you are currently using. For example, if you are working in a table, table tools will appear. There are thirty-two different Property Bars.

♦ **Application Bar**. Information about the document currently open in WordPerfect, including filename, printer selection, and insertion point status.

We will examine many of these tools and features in later chapters of this book.

TYPING TEXT

When typing a document in WordPerfect, press the Enter key only when you get to the end of a paragraph. (You can press the Enter key twice if you want an extra blank line between paragraphs.) WordPerfect takes care of the lines within a paragraph. If the word you are typing will not fit entirely on the current line, WordPerfect will go to the next line. This feature is called *word wrap.* A short line of text—a date or greeting like "Dear Mr. Smith"—counts as a paragraph all by itself.

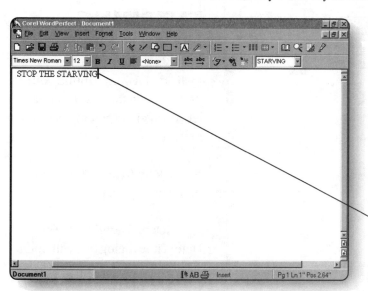

1. **Type** some **text**—your company name, for example—on the top line of the new document.

If you make any mistakes while typing, you can press the Backspace key to erase any letter to the left of the blinking insertion point.

2. **Press** the **Enter key**. The insertion point will move to the next line.

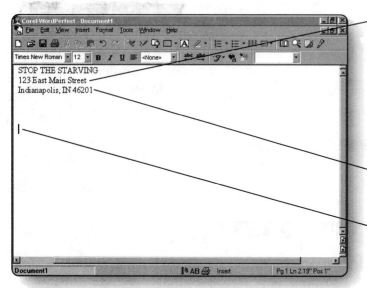

3. **Type** your **address** on the second line.

4. **Press** the **Enter key**. A paragraph mark will be inserted, turning the line into a complete paragraph.

5. **Type** your **city, state,** and **zip code** on the third line.

6. **Press** the **Enter key four more times**. Four empty lines will be created.

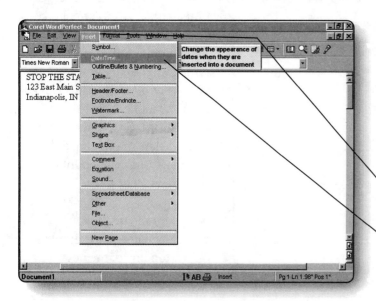

ENTERING DATE TEXT

Instead of fishing around your desk looking for your calendar, let WordPerfect put today's date in your letter for you.

1. **Click** on **Insert**. The Insert menu will appear.

2. **Click** on **Date/Time**. The Date/Time dialog box will open.

3. **Click** on the **Date/Time format** you would like to use in your letter.

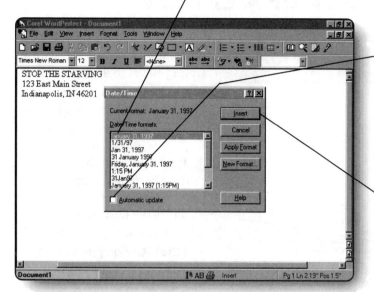

4. **Click** on **Insert**. The Date/Time dialog box will close and the current date will be inserted into your document.

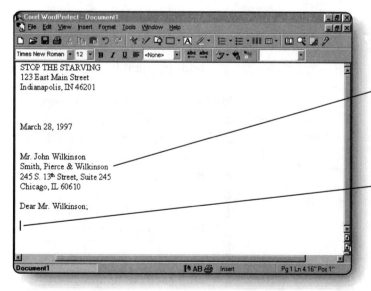

5. **Press** the **Enter key three more times** to move down your document.

6. **Type** the **name, address,** and **salutation** of the person to receive your letter. Press the Enter key as needed.

7. **Press** the **Enter key twice**, after typing the salutation line, to position the insertion point further down the page.

ENTERING THE
BODY OF A LETTER

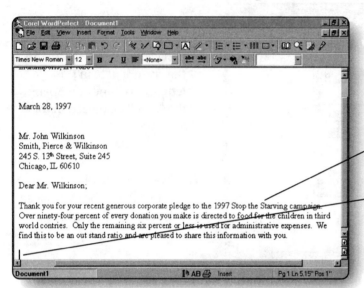

Now is the time word wrap will come into play. Just keep typing when you get to the right side of your screen. Don't worry, WordPerfect will do its job and arrange the paragraph for you.

1. Type a **paragraph** of text for the first body paragraph.

2. Press the **Enter key twice**. A blank line will be inserted and the insertion point will be moved to the beginning of a new paragraph.

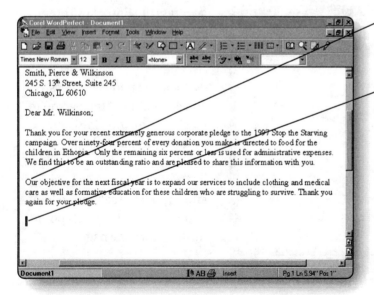

3. Type another **paragraph** of text to serve as the second body paragraph.

4. Press the **Enter key twice**. A blank line will be inserted and the insertion point will move to the beginning of a new paragraph.

5. Type any **remaining text** for the body of the letter.

6. Press the **Enter key twice** after each paragraph.

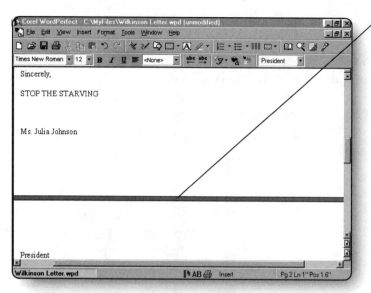

Some of the features we will be discussing in the next several chapters only work when you have more than one page of text, so I recommend that you type several paragraphs here, enough to flow to a second page. You can tell that you have reached a second page when you see a gray line appear on your screen. The gray line is called a *page break*.

ADDING A SPECIAL CHARACTER

WordPerfect has many special symbols you can use in your document. You'll find the registered trademark symbol, the copyright symbol, a bunch of multinational alphabet characters, and many that are just plain fun to use.

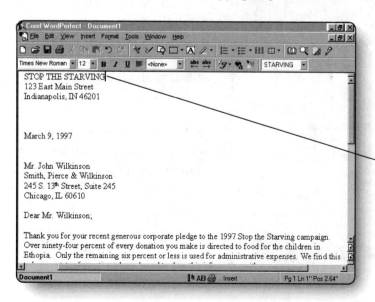

1. **Press** and **hold** the **Ctrl key,** and then **press** the **Home key.** The insertion point will move to the top of your document.

2. **Click** the **mouse button once** at the location where you want the special symbol placed. The insertion point will move to that point.

3. **Click** on **Insert**. The Insert menu will appear.

4. **Click** on **Symbol**. The WordPerfect Characters dialog box will open. WordPerfect has over 2,400 special characters available in 15 different categories, including mathematical, multinational, Greek, and Japanese.

TIP

You can go straight to the WordPerfect Character dialog box by pressing Ctrl+W. Ctrl+W is called a *shortcut key*. Most WordPerfect functions have shortcut keys that let you bypass the menus once you get used to them.

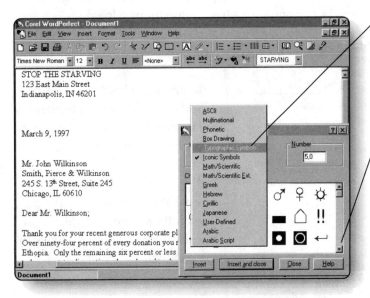

5. **Click** on **Typographic Symbols** or one of the other categories from the Character set drop-down box. A different selection of symbols will appear in the Characters: scroll box.

6. **Scroll down** the Characters: scroll box until you see the desired symbol.

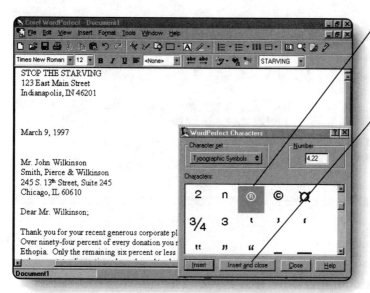

7. **Click** on the **symbol** you want placed in your letter. The selected symbol will have a dotted box around it.

8. **Click** on **Insert and close**. The WordPerfect Character dialog box will disappear.

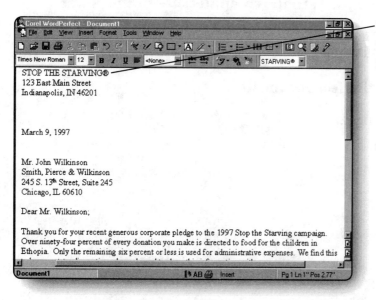

The symbol will be inserted into your document at the insertion point.

2 Saving Documents and Closing WordPerfect

When you work on a document in WordPerfect, the changes you make go into a temporary copy in your computer's memory. That memory gets erased when you turn the computer off—or the power fails. To avoid losing your document, you need to save it as a file. In this chapter, you'll learn how to:

✦ Save and close a WordPerfect document

✦ Exit the WordPerfect program

SAVING A WORDPERFECT DOCUMENT

When you first create a document, it has no name. If you want to go back to that document at a later date, it must have a name so WordPerfect can find it. WordPerfect will ask for a name the first time you save the document, and after that the name you give it will appear in the Title Bar at the very top of the screen, as well as at the bottom of the screen in the Application Bar.

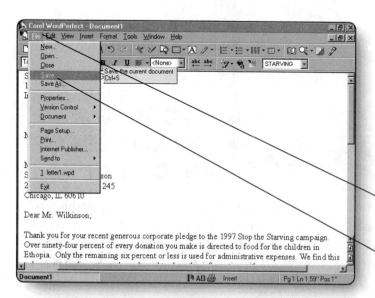

1. **Click** on **File**. The File menu will appear.

2. **Click** on **Save**. The Save File dialog box will open.

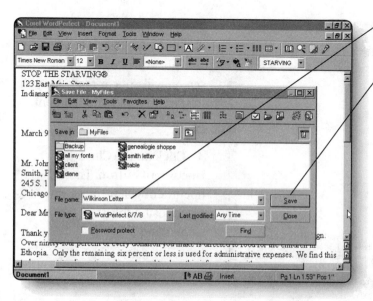

3. **Enter** a **descriptive name** for the file in the File name: list box.

4. **Click** on **Save**. The file will be saved.

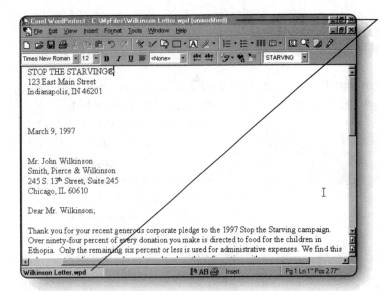

Notice the filename appears at the top and bottom of the window.

CLOSING A WORDPERFECT DOCUMENT

When you are finished working on a document you should close it. *Closing* is the equivalent of putting it away for later use. When you close a document, you are only putting the document away—not the program. WordPerfect is still active and ready to work for you.

1. **Click** on **File**. The File menu will appear.

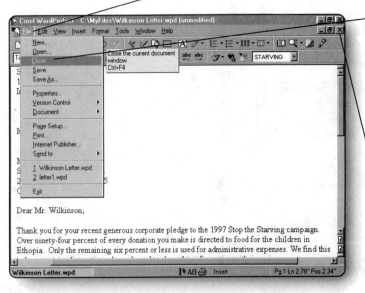

2. **Click** on **Close**. The document will be put away and another WordPerfect blank screen will appear ready for you to start on another document.

OR

3. **Click** on the **Close Document button.** The document will be put away. By choosing this step, you skip steps 1 and 2.

EXITING THE WORDPERFECT PROGRAM

If you are finished working with WordPerfect, exit the WordPerfect program. This procedure will protect your data and avoid possible program damage.

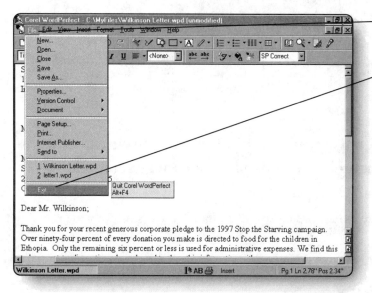

1. **Click** on **File**. The File menu will appear.

2. **Click** on **Exit**. The WordPerfect program will close and you will return to the Windows 95 desktop.

OR

3. **Click** on the **Close Program button.** The WordPerfect program will be put away. By choosing this step, you skip steps 1 and 2.

NOTE

If you still have an unsaved file open, WordPerfect will ask if you want to save it. If you do want to save the file, click on Yes; if you do not want to save it, click on No. You do not have to close a file before you exit the WordPerfect program. WordPerfect will close the document as you exit the program.

3 Opening and Editing a Document

It is time to go back and finish working on your letter. To edit a document you have already closed, you must open that document again. In this chapter, you'll learn how to:

✦ Open an existing WordPerfect document

✦ Insert, select, delete, and move text

✦ Reverse mistakes with Undo

✦ Use the Find and Replace feature

✦ Move around in a WordPerfect document

OPENING A WORDPERFECT DOCUMENT

When you open a file, you are pulling a copy of that file up into the computer's memory so you can continue to work on it. After you make any changes, be sure to save the file again.

1. **Start** the **WordPerfect program**, if you have not already done so.

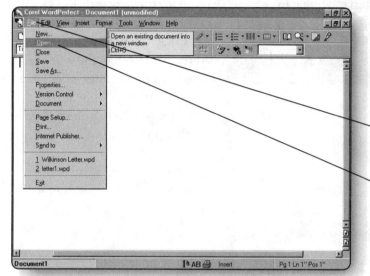

2. **Click** on **File**. The File menu will appear.

3. **Click** on **Open**. The Open dialog box will open.

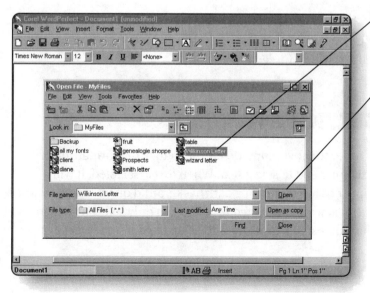

4. **Click** on the **name** of the file you wish to open. The filename will be highlighted.

5. **Click** on **Open**. The file will be placed on your screen, ready for you to edit.

INSERTING TEXT

WordPerfect begins in *insert* mode. This means that when you want to add new text to a document, simply place the insertion point where you want the new text to be and start typing. WordPerfect will push the existing text to the right and keep moving it over to make room for the new text.

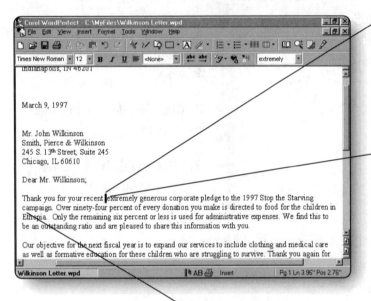

1. **Click** the **mouse pointer** directly in front of the word in the body of the letter where you want new text to appear. The blinking insertion point will go to that position.

2. **Type** any new **word** or **phrase**, adding a space before or after as necessary.

Notice how the words that were previously at the end of the line you began typing on no longer fit on the first line and drop down to the second line.

SELECTING TEXT

In order to move, copy, delete, or change the formatting of text, you need to select text. When text is selected, it will appear as light type on a dark background on your screen, just the reverse of unselected text. You can only select a sequential block of text at a time, not bits of text in different places.

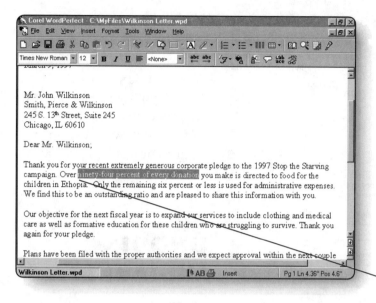

The following list shows different selection techniques:

✦ To select one word, click twice on the word.

✦ To select a sentence, click three times on the sentence.

✦ To select a paragraph, click four times on the paragraph.

✦ To select an entire document, press Ctrl+A.

✦ To select a block of text, click at the beginning of the text. Then press and hold the mouse button and drag across the text until you get to the end of the text you want to select. Finally, release the mouse button.

NOTE

To deselect text, click the mouse pointer anywhere in the document where the text is not highlighted. The text will be deselected.

DELETING TEXT

You can delete unwanted text one character, one word, one sentence, one paragraph, one page at a time, or any combination of the above. It is a good idea to save your file before you delete anything, in case you accidentally delete the wrong text. (But the Undo feature—introduced in the next section—makes it fairly safe to go ahead without saving the file!)

1. **Click** on the **Save button**. The file will be saved.

2. **Select** the **text** to be deleted.

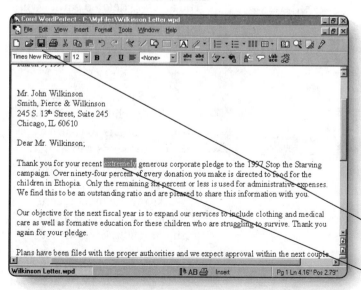

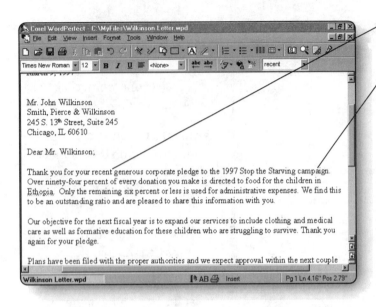

3. **Press** the **Delete key**. The text will be deleted.

Notice that as soon as the deleted text disappears, any text below or to the right of the deleted words will move up to remove any blank space.

UNDOING MISTAKES

WordPerfect has a wonderful feature called *Undo*. This feature will reverse the last step you performed. In fact, it can even reverse the last 10 steps you performed!

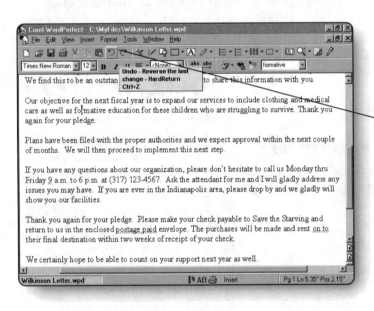

1. **Click** on the **Undo button**. The text you deleted earlier will be restored.

NOTE

To undo multiple steps at one time, click on Edit and then Undo/Redo History. Select the steps you want to reverse and click on Undo. Unfortunately, this only works for the most recent steps—you cannot undo the fifth step back without also undoing the last four things you executed.

USING FIND AND REPLACE

Use Find and Replace to search for any text, such as phrases, words, or individual characters in a document. You can replace some or all occurrences of the text with other text, or you can delete the text.

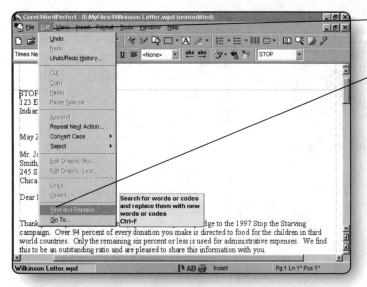

1. **Click** on **Edit**. The Edit menu will appear.

2. **Click** on **Find and Replace**. The Find and Replace dialog box will open.

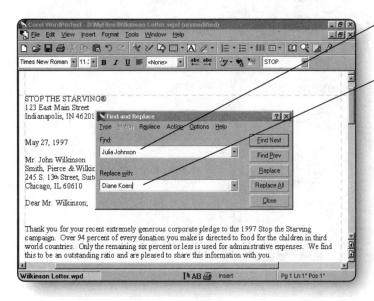

3. **Type** the **text** you want to find in the Find: list box.

4. **Type** the **text** you want to replace the Find text with in the Replace with: list box.

5. **Click** on the **Match** in the Find and Replace dialog box. The Match menu will appear. This menu offers choices for the text for which you are searching.

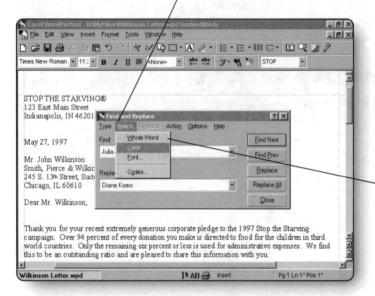

In a Whole Word match, the replacement occurs only when the text is a word, not part of a word. For example, to change "and" to "also," select Whole Word so that words such as "band" or "Anderson" are not changed.

6. **Click** on **Whole Word,** if desired.

Case finds only text that matches the upper- and lowercase letters you type. If you type "Adam" and select Case, you will not find "adam."

7. **Click** on **Case,** if desired.

Font finds text with specific typeface, style, size, and attributes (such as bold or shadow).

8. **Click** on **Font.** The Match Font dialog box will open.

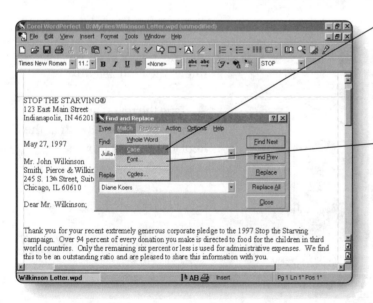

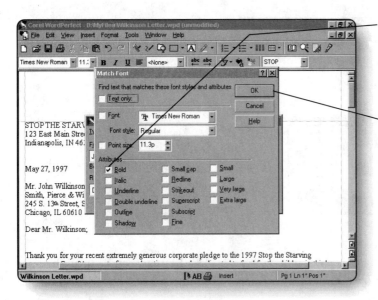

9. **Click** on the **font** or **attributes** for which you are searching. A ✔ will be placed next to the options you choose.

10. **Click** on **OK**. The Match Font dialog box will close.

A notation of your selection appears below the Find: list box.

TIP

If you want to replace text with different fonts, click on Replace and then Fonts. Select replacement fonts and attributes from the Replace Font dialog box.

11. **Click** on **Find Next** to search forward in the document, or **click** on **Find Prev** to search backward in the document. WordPerfect will find and highlight the first occurrence of the found text.

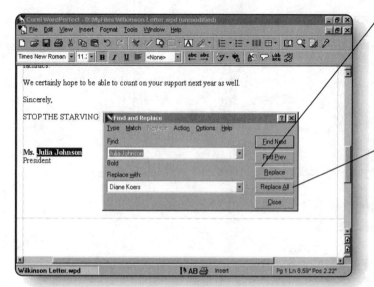

12. **Click** on **Replace**. WordPerfect will replace the text and jump to the next occurrence.

13. **Repeat step 12** until the document has been searched. When no more occurrences of the Find: text is located, a message box will appear advising you that the Find: text is not found.

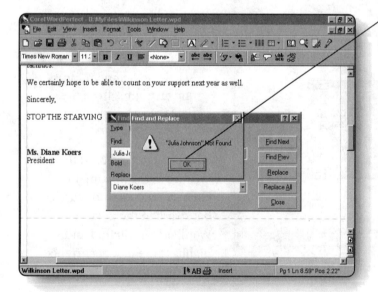

14. **Click** on **OK.** The message box will close.

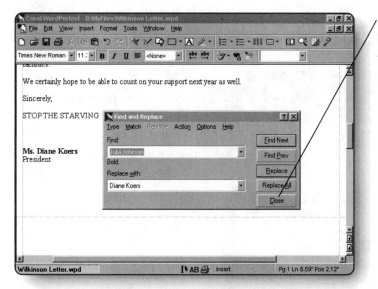

15. **Click** on **Close.** The Find and Replace dialog box will close.

CUTTING AND PASTING

Windows 95 comes with a feature called the *Clipboard*, which lets you hold information temporarily. It is extremely helpful if you want to move text from one place to another. To move information, you can use two features called *cut* and *paste*.

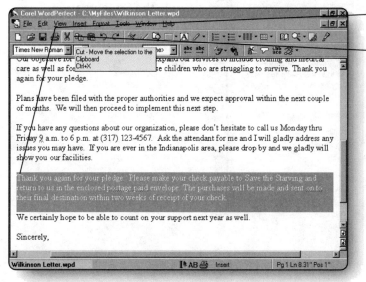

1. **Select** the **text** to be moved.

2. **Click** on the **Cut button.** The text will be removed from the document, but it's not really gone. It's being held on the Windows Clipboard.

3. **Position** the **insertion point** where you want the text to be moved.

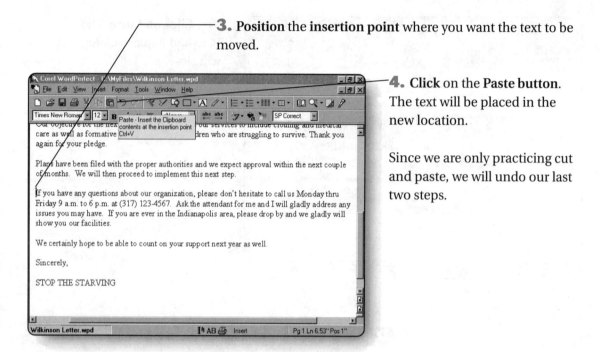

4. **Click** on the **Paste button**. The text will be placed in the new location.

Since we are only practicing cut and paste, we will undo our last two steps.

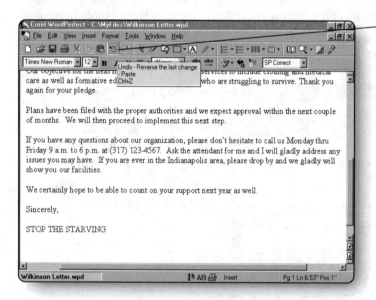

5. **Click twice** on the **Undo button**—once to undo the Paste operation and the second time to undo the Cut operation. The text will be back where it was before we started this section.

MOVING AROUND IN A DOCUMENT

As you've seen, you can work on any part of the document that shows on your screen simply by clicking the mouse pointer where you want to be. You can also move around in a WordPerfect document by pressing the Up, Down, Right, or Left Arrow keys on your keyboard.

There are several shortcut keys designed to speed up the process of moving around in a WordPerfect document. The mini-table illustrates these shortcut keys.

To Move	Do This
A word at a time	Press Ctrl+Right Arrow or Ctrl+Left Arrow
A paragraph at a time	Press Ctrl+Up Arrow or Ctrl+Down Arrow
A full screen up at a time	Press the PageUp key
A full screen down at a time	Press the PageDown key
To the beginning of a line	Press the Home key
To the end of a line	Press the End key
To the top of a document	Press Ctrl+Home
To the bottom of a document	Press Ctrl+End
To a specified page number in a document	Press Ctrl+G, and then enter the page number

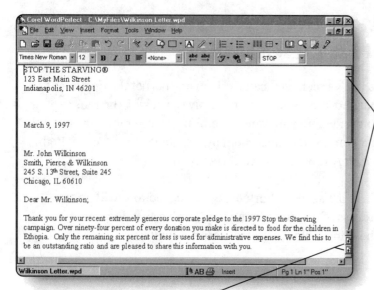

You can also use the scroll bar at the right side of the screen to get around your document very quickly.

1. **Click once** on the **horizontal scroll bar arrows** on the right side of the screen to move up or down a line at a time.

2. **Click** the **mouse pointer** at the location where you want the insertion point placed.

3. **Click** on the **Next Page** or **Previous Page buttons**. You will move through the document one page at a time.

4. **Click** the **mouse pointer** at the location where you want the insertion point placed.

4 Printing Letters and Envelopes

Now that your letter is complete, it is time to print it. *Print* means "send it somewhere"—not necessarily to your printer. You can print it to your printer for a hard copy of the document, or you can print it to your fax/modem to send it directly to the recipient. In this chapter, you'll learn how to:

✦ Make a document the size you want

✦ Print a document

✦ Fax a document from your computer

✦ Create an envelope

✦ Save a return address for future use

✦ Select an envelope size

MAKING IT FIT

Use the Make It Fit feature to make a document fit a certain number of pages. For example, you can take a letter that is more than one page and shrink it to fit just on one page or you can expand it to fill two pages. Depending upon the permissions you give when you use this feature, items that WordPerfect can adjust include margins, font size, and line spacing.

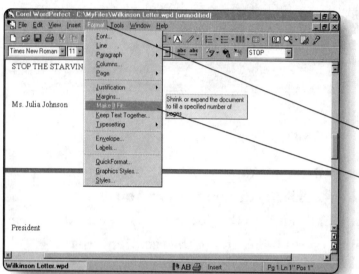

1. **Click** on **Format**. The Format menu will appear.

2. **Click** on **Make It Fit**. The Make It Fit dialog box will open.

The dialog box shows the current number of pages in your document. In the Desired number of pages: box, you can enter the number of pages you want the document to be. You can also choose which items to adjust to make it fit.

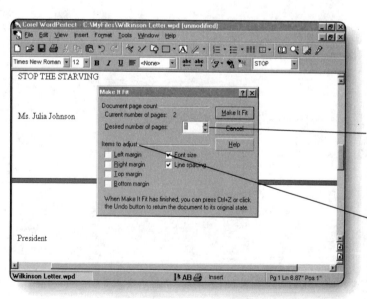

3. **Click** on the **up and down arrows** (◆) next to the Desired number of pages: box to set the number of pages.

4. **Click** on **your choices** in the Items to adjust area. A ✔ will be placed next to each selected option.

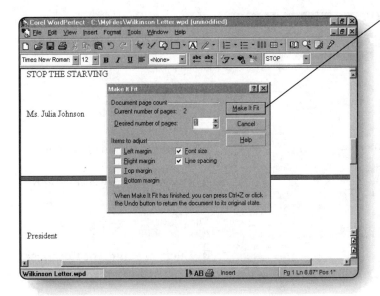

5. **Click** on **Make It Fit**. The document will be compressed or expanded as you requested.

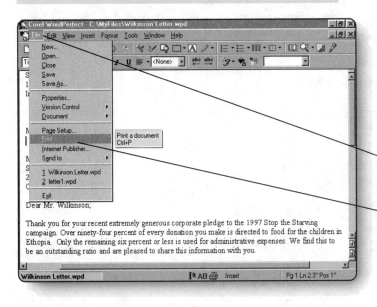

FAXING A DOCUMENT

If you have a fax/modem installed and working in your computer you can send a document to anyone who has a fax/modem or fax machine at their location.

1. **Click** on **File**. The File menu will appear.

2. **Click** on **Print**. The Print dialog box will open.

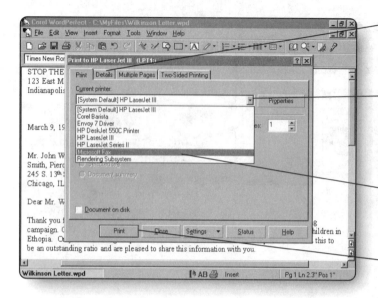

3. Click on the **Printer tab,** if necessary. The Printer tab will come to the top of the stack.

4. Click on the **down arrow** (▼) to the right of the Current printer: list box. A list of available printers will appear.

5. Click on the **fax system** you have installed on your computer.

6. Click on **Print**. The Compose New Fax dialog box will open.

NOTE

If you are using Microsoft Fax, follow steps 7 through 15 to complete the Fax Wizard. If you are using another fax system, skip to the next section, "Faxing with Software other than Microsoft Fax."

After a few seconds, a dialog box will open asking you for information. The choices you see will vary depending upon the type of fax software you have installed.

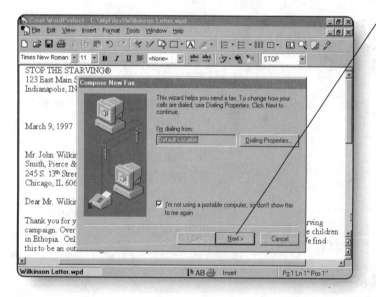

7. Click on **Next**. The fax recipient information box will open.

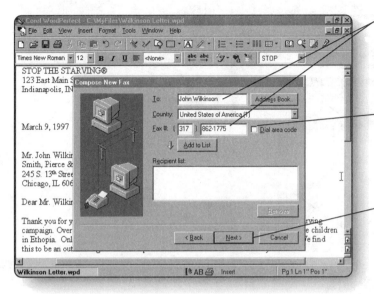

8. Type the **name** and **telephone number** of the recipient in the appropriate locations.

9. Click on **Dial area code**, if you are calling long distance. A ✔ will be placed in the check box.

10. Click on **Next**.

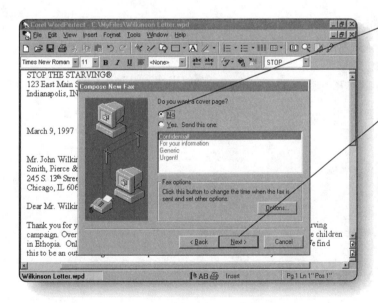

11. Click on **Yes** or **No** to answer the question about a cover page. If you select Yes, specify which cover page to use.

12. Click on **Next**. The cover page box will open.

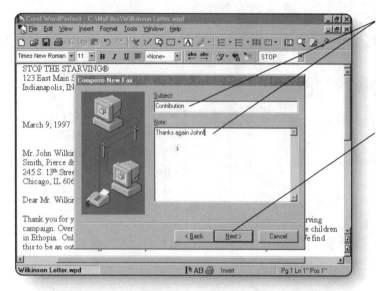

13. Type the **subject** and **note information**, if you are sending a cover page. If you are not sending a cover page, leave this blank.

14. Click on **Next**.

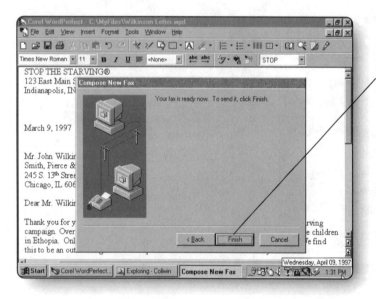

You are now ready to send the fax.

15. Click on **Finish**.

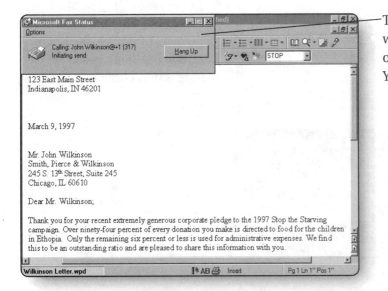

The Microsoft Fax Status window will open, updating you on the status of sending the fax. Your faxing is now complete.

Faxing with Software other than Microsoft Fax

Most fax programs ask for similar kinds of information, and are very easy to use. The following example assumes you are using WinFax as your faxing software. If you have a different program, the figures will look somewhat different, but you should still be able to follow steps like these:

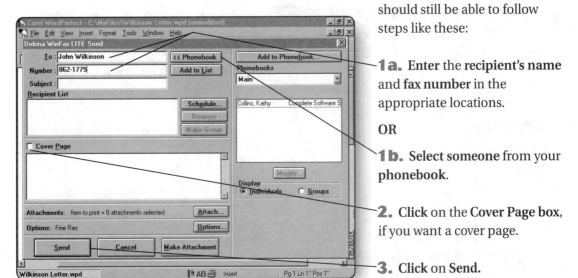

1a. Enter the **recipient's name** and **fax number** in the appropriate locations.

OR

1b. Select **someone** from your **phonebook**.

2. Click on the **Cover Page box**, if you want a cover page.

3. Click on **Send**.

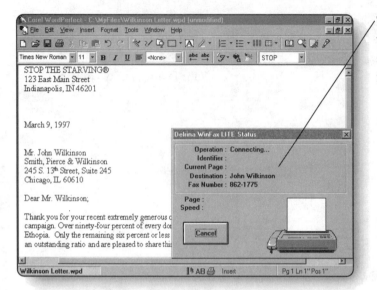

The WinFax Status dialog box will open, updating you on the status of sending the fax. Your faxing is now complete.

PRINTING A DOCUMENT

If you want a paper copy of your document to send to the recipient or a copy for your records, you also use the Print feature of WordPerfect.

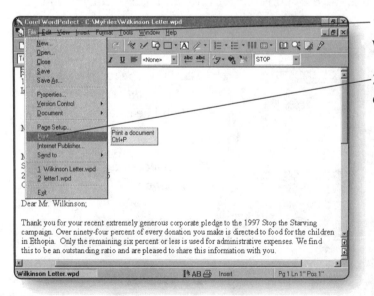

1. **Click** on **File**. The File menu will appear.

2. **Click** on **Print**. The Print dialog box will open.

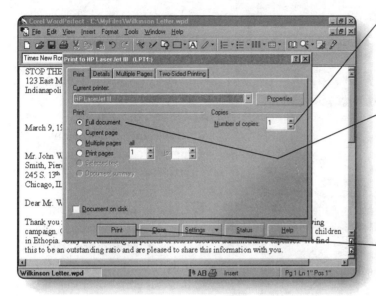

3. Click on the **up and down arrow** (◆) next to the Number of copies: box to choose the number of copies to print.

4. Click on an **option button** in the Print area to select what you want to print: the entire document, the current page, a range of pages, or multiple pages.

5. Click on **Print**. The document will be sent to your printer.

CREATING AN ENVELOPE

Creating an envelope is easy in WordPerfect. If you are typing a letter, WordPerfect will often recognize how the envelope should be addressed.

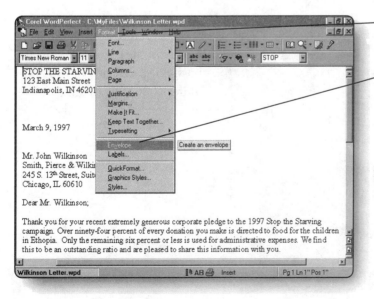

1. Click on **Format**. The Format menu will appear.

2. Click on **Envelope**. The Envelope dialog box will open.

If WordPerfect was able to recognize where to send the letter, the name will appear in the Mailing Addresses area. If it does not appear, or is incorrect, you will need to type it in yourself.

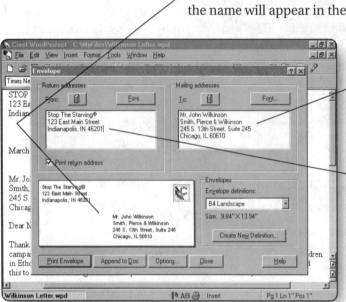

3. **Click** in the **Mailing Addresses box** and **type** any **changes** needed to the name and address.

4. **Click** in the **Return Addresses box** and **type** in the desired **return address**, if you want WordPerfect to put a return address on your envelope.

Saving the Return Address

If you want to save the return address for future use, you can add it to your Corel Address Book.

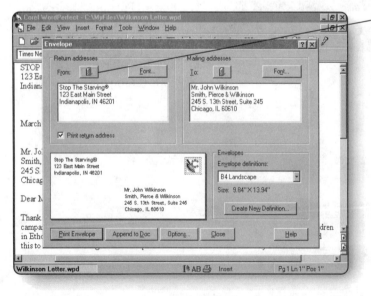

1. **Click** on the **Address Book button** on the upper left side of the dialog box. The Corel Address Book will open.

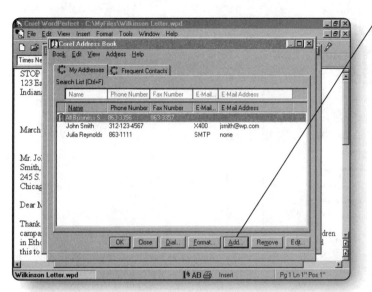

2. **Click** on **Add**. The New Entry dialog box will open.

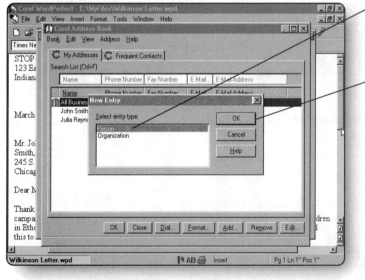

3. **Click** on **Person** or **Organization**. The item will be highlighted.

4. **Click** on **OK**. The New Person dialog box will open.

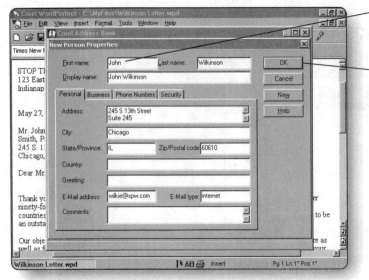

5. **Fill in** any available **information** in this dialog box.

6. **Click** on **OK**. The person or organization will be added to your address book.

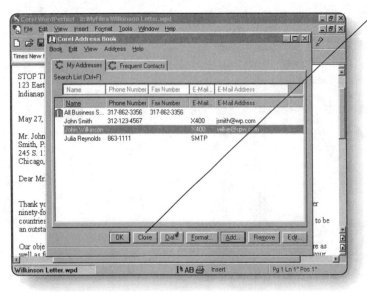

7. **Click** on **Close.** The address book will close and you will be returned to your envelope.

Selecting an Envelope Size

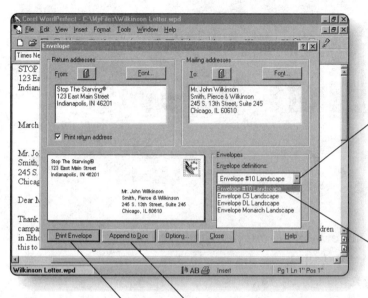

By default, WordPerfect assumes you want a standard #10 business envelope. If that is not the case, you can choose from a variety of sizes.

1. **Click** on the **down arrow (▼)** next to the Envelope definitions: list box. A list of available envelope sizes will appear. (Your choices may vary with different printer selections.)

2. **Click** on the desired **envelope size**. You are now ready to finish the envelope.

3a. **Click** on **Append to Doc**, if you want to print the envelope later.

OR

3b. **Click** on **Print Envelope**. The envelope will be printed.

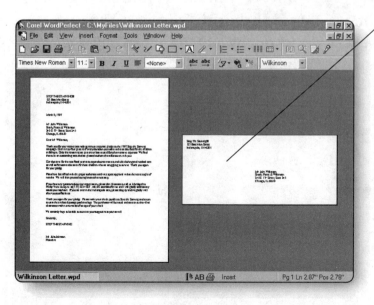

When you choose Append to Doc, the envelope will be added to the bottom of your document. With your current settings, it will show up on your screen as a page following the page of text. This figure gives you a sneak preview of Chapter 5, which discusses the different ways WordPerfect can show you your document.

5 Working with Views

WordPerfect gives you several different perspectives on your document. When you first install the program, it shows your documents in Page view. Page view lets you see your document as it will look on a printout, with all its headers and footers, footnotes, page numbering, and margins. You can change this default to Draft view, either for one document or for everything you do. If you have used earlier DOS versions of WordPerfect, Draft view is very similar to what you may have used—just the text, without the running headers and other items that show up on the printed pages. You can also see a whole page, or check the layout by looking at two pages at a time. In this chapter, you'll learn how to:

✦ Switch from Page view to Draft view

✦ View two pages at a time

✦ Make Draft view the default view

✦ Zoom to Full Page view

✦ Zoom in for a closer look

✦ Use the shadow cursor

SWITCHING FROM PAGE VIEW TO DRAFT VIEW

Draft view is similar to Page view except that you cannot see your headers and footers, footnotes, page numbering, or margins. Some people prefer Draft view because it gives them more room on the screen to see their text.

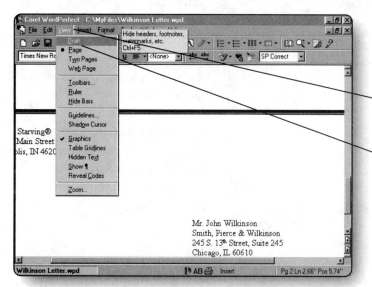

1. **Click** on **View**. The View menu will appear.

2. **Click** on **Draft**. The view will change to Draft view.

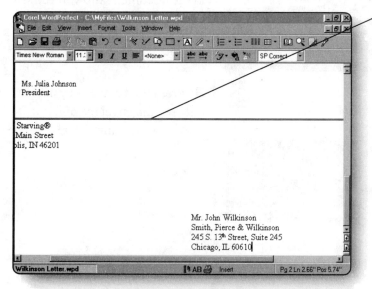

As you scroll down in your document to look at the differences between the two views, do you notice the difference in the page break?

VIEWING TWO PAGES AT A TIME

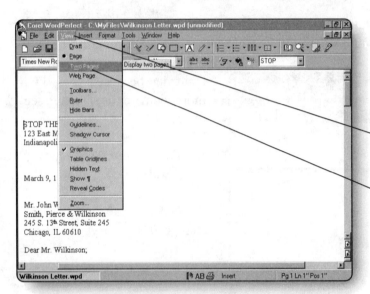

Sometimes it helps to see your pages side by side. This can help you in checking that your document has an overall balanced and consistent look to it.

1. **Click** on **View**. The View menu will appear.

2. **Click** on **Two Pages**. The view will change to Two Page view. You will see the current page your insertion point is on and the page facing it.

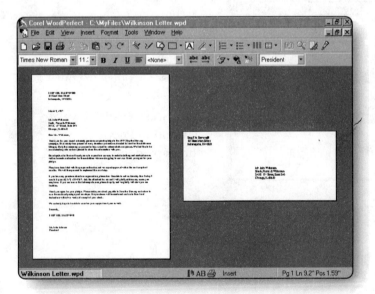

Two Page view is editable, so you have a blinking insertion point in the document and you could continue to type or edit in this view. (That is, if you could actually read the text.)

3. **Press** the **PageUp key**, if you only see the envelope and not the accompanying letter.

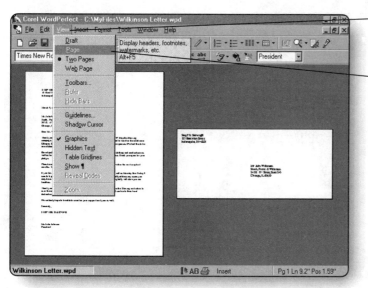

4. Click on **View**. The View menu will appear.

5. Click on **Page**. The view will be restored to the default Page view.

MAKING DRAFT VIEW THE DEFAULT VIEW

If you decide you like the extra screen space you get with the Draft view, you can make it the default view. That way, each time you start WordPerfect your documents will appear in Draft view.

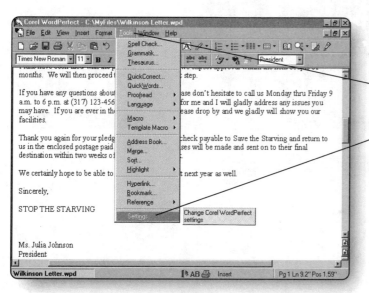

1. Click on **Tools**. The Tools menu will appear.

2. Click on **Settings**. The Settings box will open.

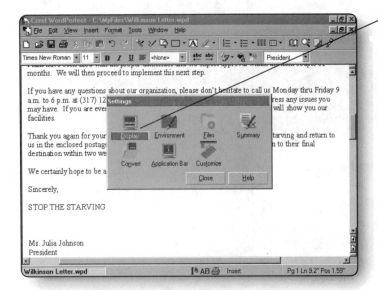

3. **Double-click** on **Display**. The Display Settings dialog box will open.

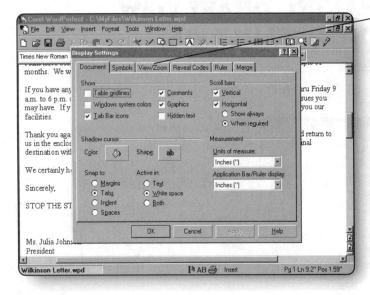

4. **Click** on the **View/Zoom tab**. The View/Zoom tab will come to the top of the stack.

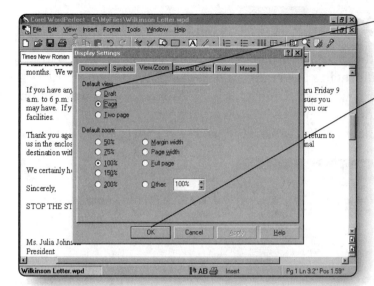

5. **Click** on **Draft** in the Default view area. The option will be selected.

6. **Click** on **OK**. The dialog box will close.

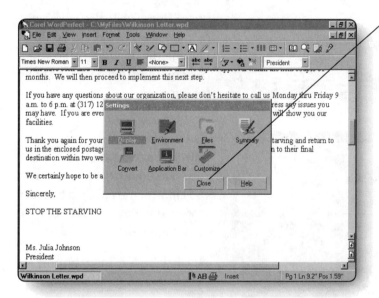

7. **Click** on **Close**. You will be returned to your document screen, in Draft view.

ZOOMING TO FULL PAGE VIEW

Another perspective that I find extremely helpful is to view my document in a Full Page view. This view is larger than the Two Page view, but smaller than Page or Draft view. You have a button on your Toolbar to switch you to various zoom percentages. If you have used an earlier version of WordPerfect, this is similar to the Print Preview feature you used to have.

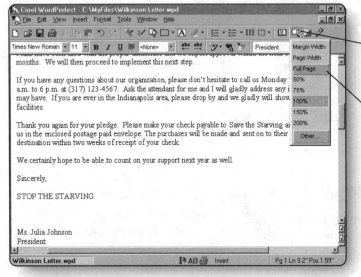

1. **Click** on the **Zoom button**. The zoom choice menu will appear.

2. **Click** on **Full Page**. Your document will be displayed one page at a time, at a size that fits each page on the screen all at once. This view is also editable, so you have a blinking insertion point in the document and you can continue to type or edit in this view.

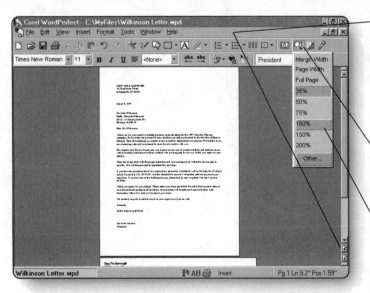

3. **Click** on the **Page Down button** to view the next page of your document. Similarly, you can click on the Page Up button to view the previous page of your document.

4. **Click** on the **Zoom button**. The zoom choice menu will appear.

5. **Click** on **100%**. The view will return to normal.

ZOOMING IN FOR A CLOSER LOOK

Occasionally you may need to take a closer look at something in your document, particularly if you are working in a very small font.

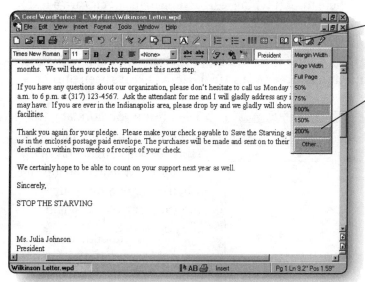

1. **Click** on the **Zoom button**. The zoom choice menu will appear.

2. **Click** on **200%**. The text on your screen will be doubled in size.

NOTE

Margin Width is a good zoom choice to use if you are printing in Landscape. Chapter 8 will discuss changing paper size or orientation so you can do this.

Your text looks larger on the screen, but it will still print in the same size you specified.

3. **Click** on the **Zoom button**. The zoom choice menu will appear.

4. **Click** on **100%**. Your screen will be restored to normal.

USING THE SHADOW CURSOR

The shadow cursor keeps your mouse pointer from getting lost. The shadow cursor shows exactly where the insertion point will go when you click the mouse. You can click anywhere to start typing text, or drag to insert clip art, a text box, or a table.

1. **Click** on the **Shadow Cursor button**. The Shadow Cursor button will be redrawn so that it looks like it's been pressed.

The I-beam you normally see when you move your mouse is replaced with a light gray line and an arrowhead that appear whenever you move your mouse over a blank spot in the document.

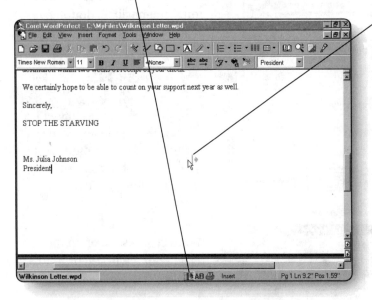

TIP

If the shadow cursor has an arrowhead on both the left and right side of the light gray line, WordPerfect is indicating this is the horizontal center of the page.

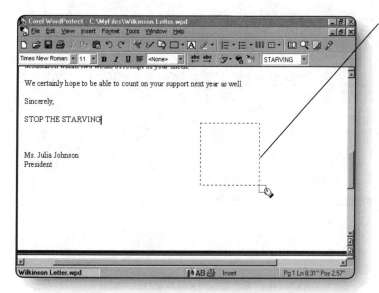

2. **Click** on the **mouse button** and **drag** a **small rectangle** on your screen.

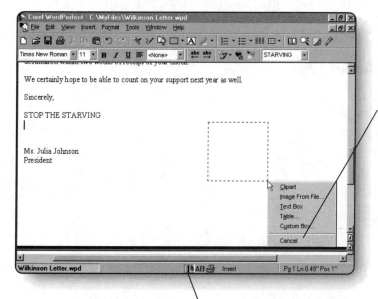

A shortcut menu will appear. From here, you can add clip art, text boxes, tables, and custom boxes.

3. **Click** on **Cancel**. The shortcut menu will close.

4. **Click** on the **Shadow Cursor button**. The shadow cursor will be turned off and the button will be redrawn in its original form.

6 Improving Your Writing

Nobody's perfect. As hard as we try to type accurately, we will make mistakes. WordPerfect has several features that can assist you in correcting errors. In this chapter, you'll learn how to:

✦ Save time with QuickWords

✦ Fix spelling errors while you type

✦ Use the Spell Checker

✦ Check your grammar

✦ Use the Thesaurus

SAVING TIME WITH QUICKWORDS

Think of QuickWords as abbreviations. Perhaps your company name or address is complicated to type. If you abbreviate it, WordPerfect can do most of the work for you—even add special formatting if you make it part of the abbreviated phrase.

1. **Type** some **text**. Press the Enter key where necessary and include any formatting you want added to the text.

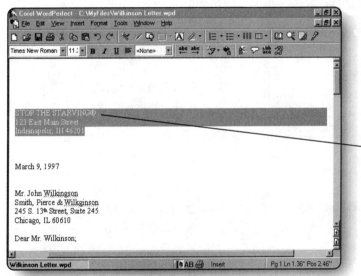

2. **Select** the **text** you just typed. The text will be highlighted.

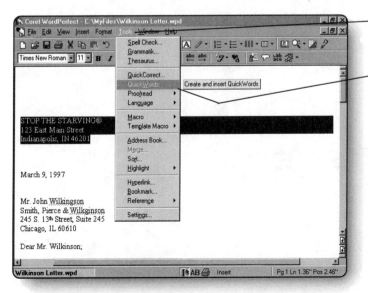

3. **Click** on **Tools**. The Tools menu will appear.

4. **Click** on **QuickWords**. The QuickCorrect dialog box will open with the QuickWords tab in the foreground.

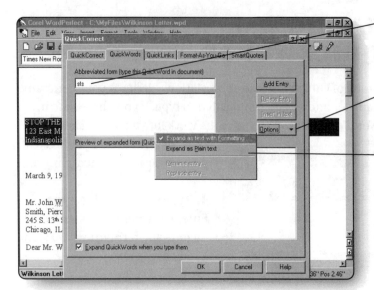

5. Type an **abbreviation** for the selected text in the Abbreviated form text box.

6. **Click** on the **Options button**. The options menu will appear.

7. **Click** on **Expand as text with Formatting** or **Expand as Plain text**.

8. **Click** on **Add Entry**. The dialog box will close.

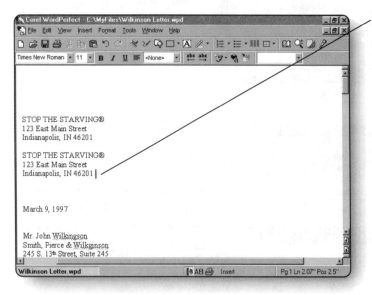

9. Type the **abbreviation** followed by a space or the Enter key. The abbreviation will be expanded.

SPELLING AS YOU GO

WordPerfect automatically checks your spelling as you type. You may notice some words have a red wavy line under them. You can correct these errors as you go along typing your text.

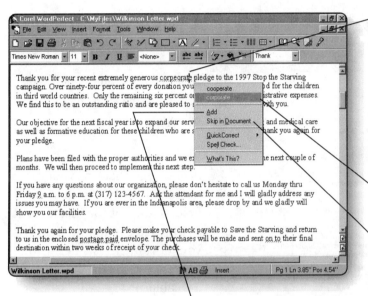

1. Position the **mouse pointer** over the misspelled word and **click** with the **right mouse button**. A shortcut menu will appear.

2. Click on **one** of the **menu choices:**

◆ Choose one of the suggested replacement words.

◆ Choose Skip in Document to tell WordPerfect to ignore this word.

◆ Choose Add to add the word to the WordPerfect dictionary for future reference.

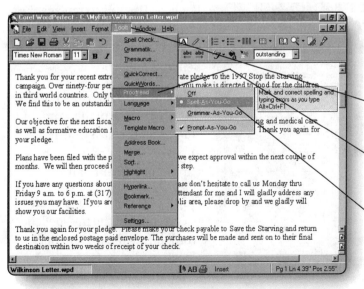

Turning Off the Spell-As-You-Go Feature:

1. Click on **Tools**. The Tools menu will appear.

2. Click on **Proofread**. A cascading menu will appear.

3. Click on **Spell-As-You-Go**. The feature will be turned off.

WORKING WITH SPELL CHECK

Instead of correcting spelling errors one at a time as you are working on the document, you can check them all at once with the Spell Check feature.

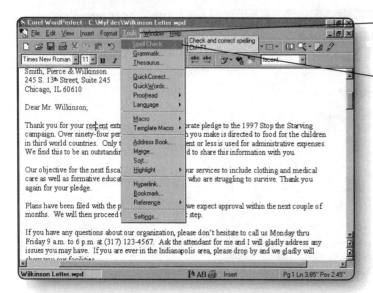

1. **Click** on **Tools**. The Tools menu will appear.

2. **Click** on **Spell Check**. The language tools dialog box will open.

WordPerfect automatically begins spell checking your document and will stop at the first misspelling, duplicate word, or irregular capitalization in your document. The next two figures describe the options available.

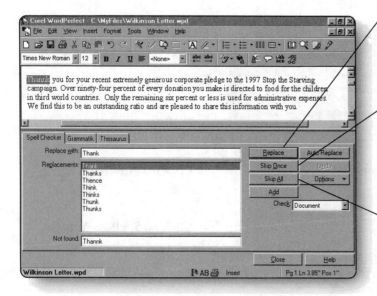

Replace Use this to replace the incorrect word with one you have selected from the Replacements: box.

Skip Once Use this to ignore this occurrence of the word, but stop again the next time it appears. This pertains to the current document only.

Skip All Use this to ignore all occurrences of the misspelled word during the current Spell Check session only.

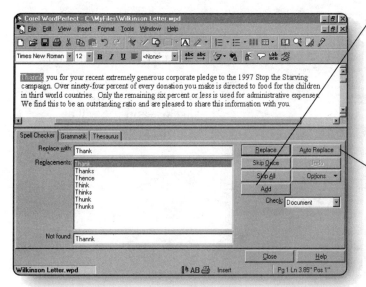

Add Use this to add the word to the supplemental dictionary. The Spell Checker will accept this word as correctly spelled in the future—so be sure you will want it in other documents before you add it to the dictionary.

Auto Replace Use this to define an automatic replacement for a word. Each time you type the misspelled word, WordPerfect will automatically replace it with the correct spelling.

If none of these options are appropriate, you will need to edit the word yourself.

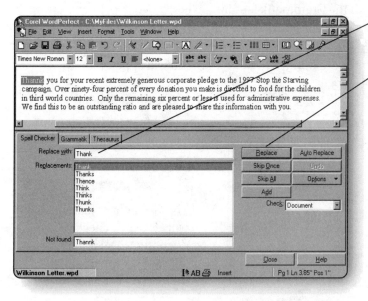

3. **Type** the **correct spelling** in the Replace with: text box.

4. **Click** on **Replace**. The misspelling will be changed.

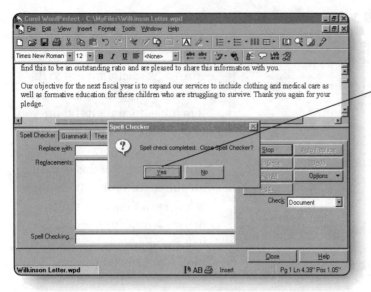

When Spell Checker is finished, you will be prompted to close the Spell Checker dialog box.

5. **Click** on **Yes**. The dialog box will close and you will be returned to your document.

CHECKING YOUR GRAMMAR

WordPerfect can correct some kinds of grammatical errors with the Grammatik feature.

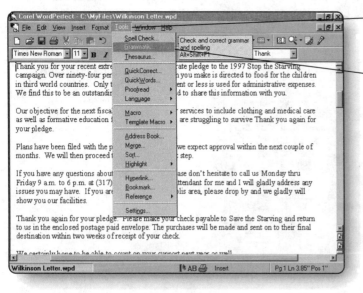

1. **Click** on **Tools**. The Tools menu will appear.

2. **Click** on **Grammatik**. The language tools dialog box will open.

NOTE

The Grammatik feature will also spell check your document. Make spelling corrections as instructed in the previous section.

Grammatik will stop at the first grammatical error and advise you of the problem at the bottom of the dialog box. It may or may not offer you replacement suggestions. If it does offer one or more suggestions, perform the following steps:

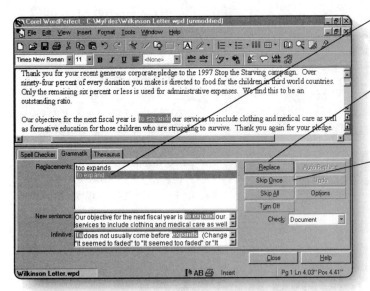

3. **Click** on the **correct suggestion** from the Replacements: list, if available.

4a. **Click** on **Replace**. The text will be changed.

OR

4b. **Click** on **Skip Once**. The proposed change will be ignored.

If Grammatik does not offer a replacement suggestion, you may need to edit the sentence manually.

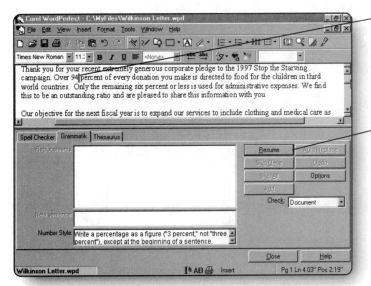

5. **Click** in the **body** of the **document** next to the correction you want to make.

6. **Type** the **correction**.

7. **Click** on **Resume** to continue the grammar check.

As with the Spell Check, you will be advised when the grammar check is complete.

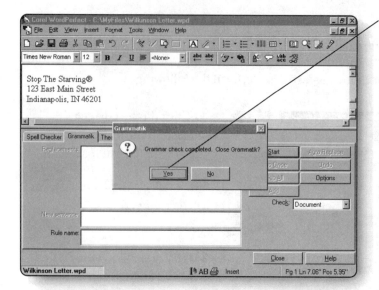

8. Click on **Yes**. The Grammatik dialog box will close.

FINDING A SYNONYM WITH THE THESAURUS

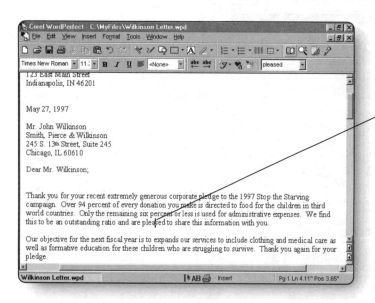

The WordPerfect Thesaurus not only gives synonyms of a word, but antonyms, definitions, and usage examples as well.

1. Position the **insertion point** in the word for which you want to find a synonym.

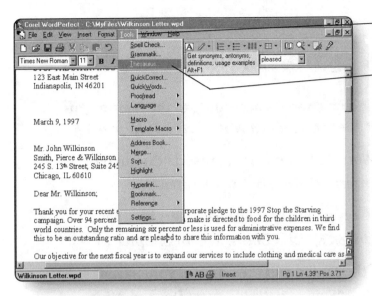

2. **Click** on **Tools**. The Tools menu will appear.

3. **Click** on **Thesaurus**. The language tools dialog box will open with definitions of your word displayed.

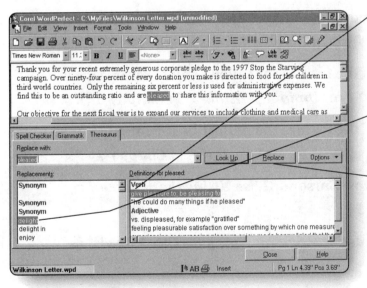

4. **Click** on the **correct definition** of your word. A list of synonyms will appear in the Replacements: scroll box.

5. **Click** on the desired **replacement word**.

6. **Click** on **Replace**. The dialog box will close and the original word will be replaced with your selection.

PART I REVIEW QUESTIONS

1.   Which item on the screen changes according to the feature you are currently using? *See "Starting WordPerfect" in Chapter 1*

2.   What feature does WordPerfect have that inserts the current date for you? *See "Entering Date Text" in Chapter 1*

3.   What is the shortcut key to add special characters into your document? *See "Adding a Special Character" in Chapter 1*

4.   What two places on the screen will the name of your saved document appear? *See "Saving a WordPerfect Document" in Chapter 2*

5.   What is one of the methods you can use to select a sentence of text? *See "Selecting Text" in Chapter 3*

6.   What is the name of the feature that allows you to reverse the last action you took? *See "Undoing Mistakes" in Chapter 3*

7.   What is the name of the feature that adjusts a document to fit a certain number of pages? *See "Making It Fit" in Chapter 4*

8.   What does the Shadow Cursor do? *See "Using the Shadow Cursor" in Chapter 5*

9.   What are QuickWords? *See "Saving Time with QuickWords" in Chapter 6*

10. Besides giving you synonyms of a word, what other types of words can the Thesaurus give you? *See "Finding a Synonym with the Thesaurus" in Chapter 6*

PART II

Formatting a Report

7 Formatting with Fonts

In the past, when people first typed letters on typewriters, there was usually only one font choice available. Later you could change fonts—if you stopped to put in a new type ball or daisy wheel. Computers make it easy to use unusual typefaces. Not only can you pick and choose the font you want, but you can also modify the size and style. In this chapter, you'll learn how to:

✦ Change the typeface, font size, and style of text

✦ Make font changes from one location

✦ Convert text to uppercase

✦ Use the Highlighter

CHANGING THE TYPEFACE

The default font for WordPerfect is normally Times New Roman, but WordPerfect comes with many additional fonts. Other software installed on your machine may give you even more fonts.

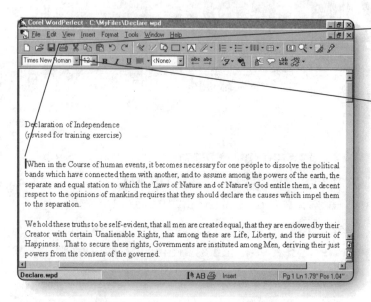

1. **Position** your **insertion point** at the location where you want the font change to begin.

2. **Click** on the **down arrow** (▼) next to the Font Face list box. A drop-down menu of your font choices will appear. As you move your mouse across the font names, you will see a sample of that typeface.

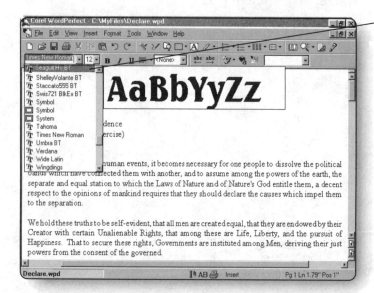

3. **Click** on the **desired font**.

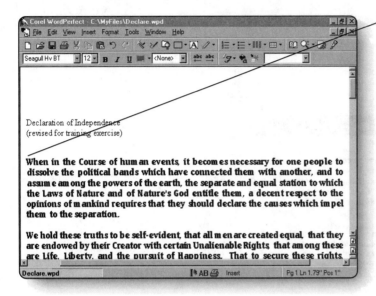

The text from the insertion point downward in your document will be changed to the new typeface.

CHANGING FONT SIZE

The default font size is a 12-point font—roughly one-sixth of an inch tall. The larger the point size of the font, the larger the text will print. Text that is 72 points is roughly one inch tall.

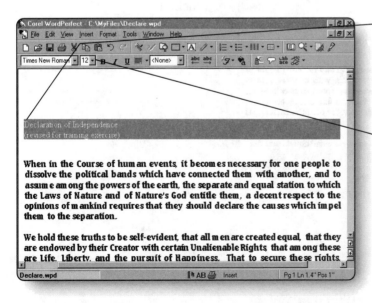

1. **Position** your **insertion point** at the location where you want the font size change to begin— or highlight the text you want to change.

2. **Click** on the **down arrow** (▼) next to the Font Size list box. A drop-down menu of available sizes will appear. These sizes may vary depending upon what typeface you are using and what printer you have installed.

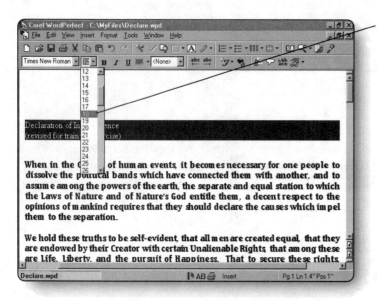

3. **Click** on the **desired size**. The text will be changed to the new size.

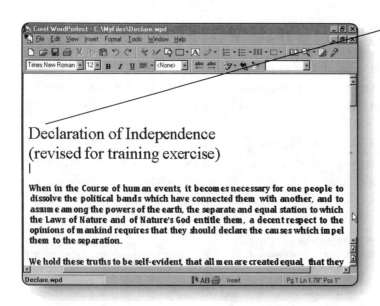

Notice how just the heading changed to the new size. The heading was selected before the size selection was made, so that's the only text WordPerfect touched.

CHANGING THE STYLE OF TEXT

The style of text includes features like **bold**, *italics*, or <u>underline</u>. You must select the text to be modified before changing the style of it.

1. **Select** the **text** you want to change.

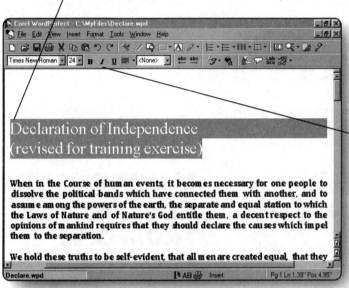

Buttons on the Property Bar make it easy to add style to your text. The button with the "b" is for **Bold**, the "i" is for *italics*, and the "u" is for <u>underline</u>.

2. **Click** on the **Bold, Italics,** or **Underline button**. The text will be changed according to your selection.

The title in this figure has both underlining and italics applied to it.

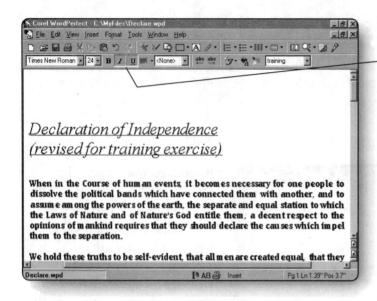

NOTE

These buttons are like toggle switches. Notice how the buttons look "pressed" if the feature is turned on. If you click one of them on and decide not to use it, click it again and the style will be turned off.

TIP

If you just want to bold, underline, or italicize a single word, you do not need to select it first. Just place the insertion point somewhere in the middle of the word and click on the desired style button.

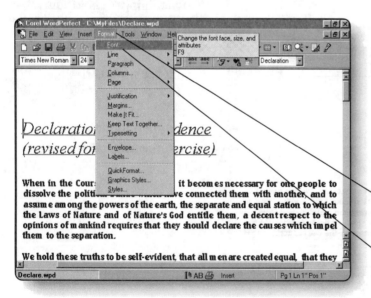

MAKING FONT CHANGES FROM ONE LOCATION

If you want to make all these types of changes at one time, you can use the Font dialog box to make your selections. This method also gives you the advantage of a Preview window to let you see an example of your selection before you actually change the text.

1. **Click** on **Format**. The Format menu will appear.

2. **Click** on **Font**. The Font dialog box will open.

3. **Select** the **items** you want to change:

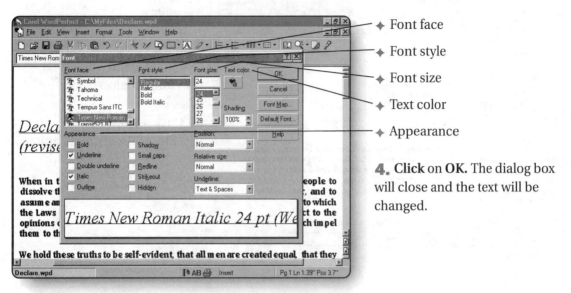

◆ Font face

◆ Font style

◆ Font size

◆ Text color

◆ Appearance

4. **Click** on **OK.** The dialog box will close and the text will be changed.

NOTE

When a style is available in Font style, it will generally give you better results than changing the appearance to get the same effect.

CHANGING THE CASE OF TEXT

Perhaps you have typed a heading to a memo, but then decided it would look better in all UPPERCASE letters. Or maybe your fingers accidentally turned on the Caps Lock key and you typed a sentence like this: tHANK YOU FOR YOUR INQUIRY. There is no need to delete this text and retype it.

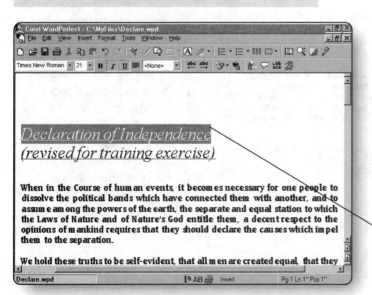

1. **Select** the **text** to be changed.

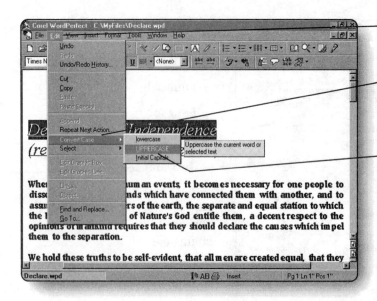

2. **Click** on **Edit**. The Edit menu will appear.

3. **Click** on **Convert Case**. A cascading menu will appear with three choices.

4. **Click** on **lowercase**, **UPPERCASE**, or **Initial Capitals**.

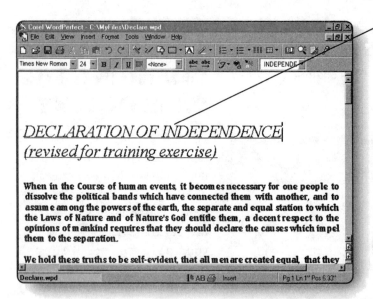

The text in this figure was changed to all UPPERCASE letters.

NOTE

You may have to manually correct a few items in the text if you have changed the text to lowercase. An example might be if you had a proper name in the middle of a sentence. WordPerfect may not recognize the first letter of that text as uppercase. Look at it carefully.

USING THE HIGHLIGHTER

Highlighting puts a bar of transparent color over text. If you have a color printer, the highlight colors will print. Black-and-white printers print the colors in gray.

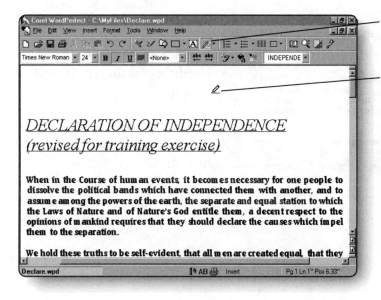

1. Click on the **Highlight button**.

Notice that the mouse pointer now looks like a small pen.

> **NOTE**
>
> If you click on the down arrow (▼) on the High-lighter button, you will be able to select the color of highlighter.

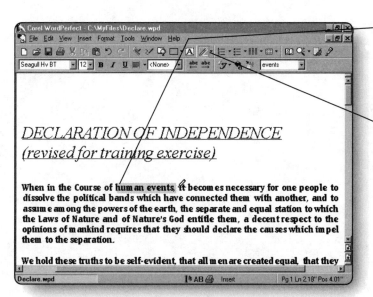

2. Click and drag the **mouse pointer** across the text to be highlighted. The text will have a yellow wash put over it.

3. Click on the **Highlight button** again to turn off the highlighter pen.

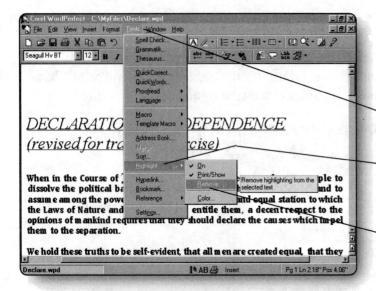

Removing Highlighting

1. **Select** the **highlighted text.**

2. **Click** on **Tools.** The Tools menu will appear.

3. **Click** on **Highlight**. The Highlight cascading menu will appear.

4. **Click** on **Remove.** The highlighting will be removed from the text.

8 Changing Paper Sizes and Margins

WordPerfect has default settings for many things, including the size of the paper and the margin settings it assumes you are using. Both of these are easy to change. In this chapter, you'll learn how to:

✦ Select a paper size and orientation

✦ Change margins

✦ Add page numbering

SELECTING A PAPER SIZE AND ORIENTATION

WordPerfect assumes you are using 8½ x 11 paper in a portrait orientation. Although this is standard for many items, you can select a different size or orientation at any point in your document.

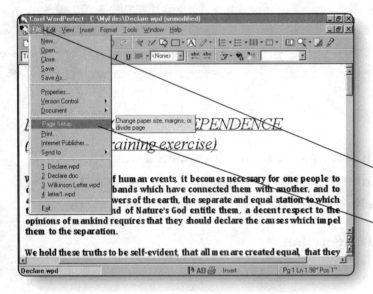

1. Position the **insertion point** at the beginning of the page where you want the new paper size setting to take effect.

2. Click on **File**. The File menu will appear.

3. Click on **Page Setup**. The Page Setup dialog box will open.

NOTE

You can also get to this same dialog box by clicking on Format, Page, and Page Setup.

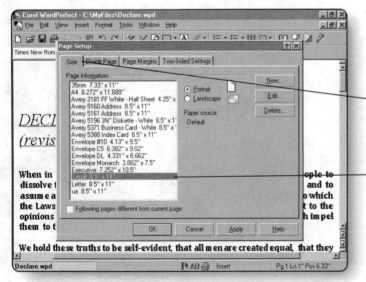

4. Click on the **Size tab**. The Size tab will come to the top of the stack.

5. Click on a **paper size** in the Page information: box.

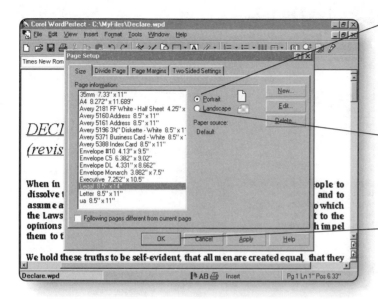

6a. **Click** on **Portrait** in the orientation area if you want the document to print in the usual vertical layout.

OR

6b. **Click** on **Landscape** in the orientation area if you want the document to print horizontally across the page.

7. **Click** on **OK**. Your document will be tagged with the print size and orientation you selected.

NOTE

You can mix and match paper sizes and orientations in a WordPerfect document. Position your insertion point at the beginning of the page you want to change, make the change as in steps 2 through 7 above, then position the insertion point where you want another change to take effect, and repeat these steps again.

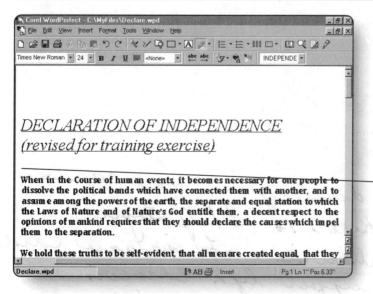

CHANGING MARGINS

The default margin settings in a WordPerfect document are one inch on each margin: left, right, top, and bottom.

1. **Position** the **insertion point** where you want the new margin setting to take effect.

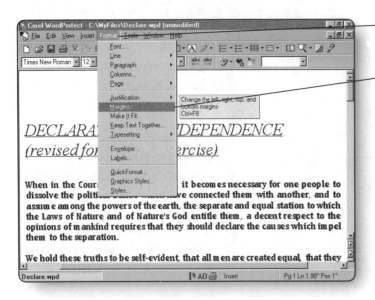

2. Click on **Format**. The Format menu will appear.

3. Click on **Margins**. The Page Setup dialog box will open.

This dialog box is the same Page Setup dialog box used in the previous section, but with the Page Margins tab in front.

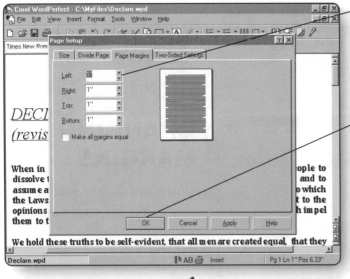

4. Click on the **up or down arrows** (◆) next to the margin you want to change until the box next to it shows your desired choice.

5. Click on **OK**. The Page Setup dialog box will close and the new settings will take effect.

*To divide page for cards
Refer to Help Topic
Page Subdivide. For instance card:
after upper left corner is set
w/ design Click Insert/New Page*

ADDING PAGE NUMBERING

Page numbering can be added to the top or bottom of the page in your document. You can also add page numbering in a header or footer. Headers and footers are discussed in Chapter 12.

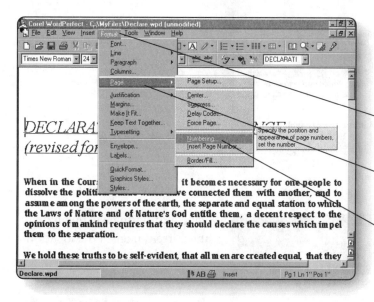

1. **Position** the **insertion point** at the beginning of the page where you want page numbering to start.

2. **Click** on **Format**. The Format menu will appear.

3. **Click** on **Page**. The Page cascading menu will appear.

4. **Click** on **Numbering**. The Select Page Numbering Format dialog box will open.

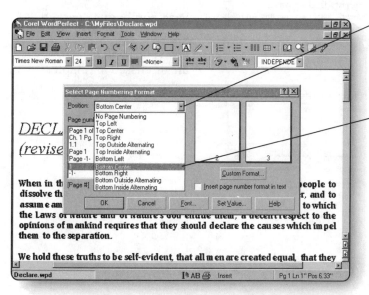

5. **Click** on the **down arrow** (▼) next to the Position: list box. A list of available choices will appear.

6. **Click** on the **location** where you want the page number to appear.

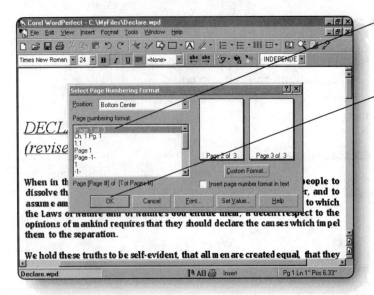

7. **Click** on a **numbering format** in the Page numbering format: scroll box.

8. **Click** on **OK**. The dialog box will close.

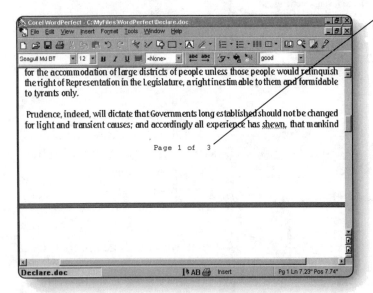

Page numbering will begin on the current page at the location you specified.

NOTE

Page numbering does not appear on the screen if you are using Draft view. Views are discussed in Chapter 5.

9 Modifying Alignment, Indentation, and Spacing

Alignment of text can be changed both horizontally and vertically to add a pleasing appearance to your document. Indentation and spacing modifications can make a document easier to read. In this chapter, you'll learn how to:

✦ Center a heading

✦ Change justification

✦ Change the indentation of a paragraph

✦ Center a page vertically

✦ Change line spacing

CENTERING A HEADING

Centering a heading of a report lets the readers know they are beginning a new section.

1. **Select** the **text** to be centered.

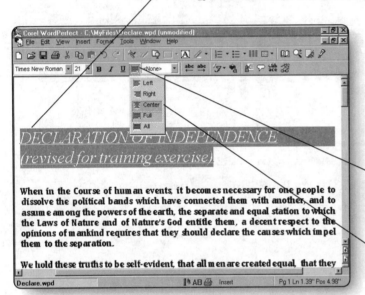

2. **Click** on the **Justification** button. A list of choices will appear.

3. **Click** on **Center**. The text you selected will be centered.

CHANGING JUSTIFICATION

Besides centering text, you can also change text so it is even on the left side (left justified), even on the right side (right justified), or even on both sides (full justified). You can even make text S T R E T C H across the page (all justified).

1. **Position** the **insertion point** where you would like the justification change to begin.

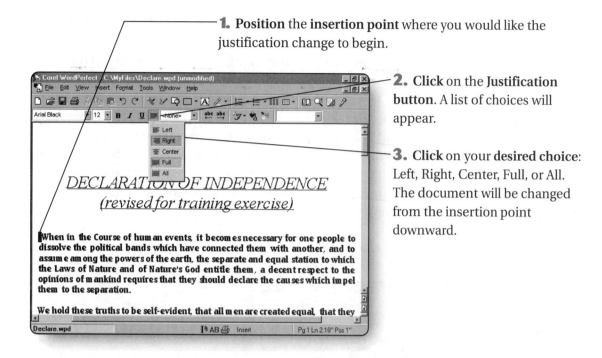

2. **Click** on the **Justification button**. A list of choices will appear.

3. **Click** on your **desired choice**: Left, Right, Center, Full, or All. The document will be changed from the insertion point downward.

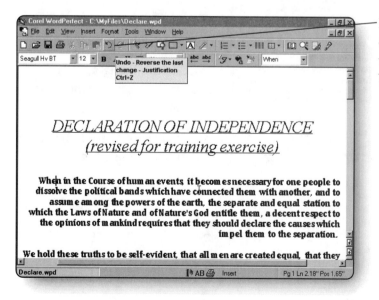

Don't forget! If you make a change you didn't want you can undo it by clicking on the Undo button on the Toolbar.

INDENTING A PARAGRAPH

Indents are very different from tabs. A tab moves just one line of text. An indent moves all the lines in a paragraph. Use Indent to move a complete paragraph one tab stop or a specified distance to the right. Use Hanging Indent to move all but the first line of a paragraph one tab stop or a specified distance to the right. A hanging indent is often used to format bibliography entries. Use Double Indent to move an entire paragraph in one tab stop from both the left and right margins. A double indent is often used to format a quotation.

1. Click at the **beginning** of the **paragraph** you want to indent.

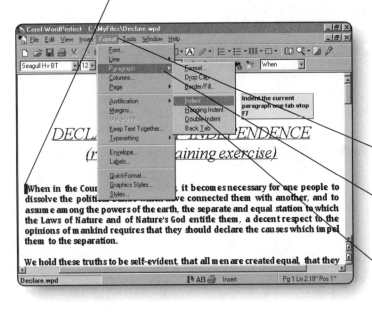

2. Click on **Format**. The Format menu will appear.

3. Click on **Paragraph**. The Paragraph cascading menu will appear.

4. Click on **Indent, Hanging Indent,** or **Double Indent.**

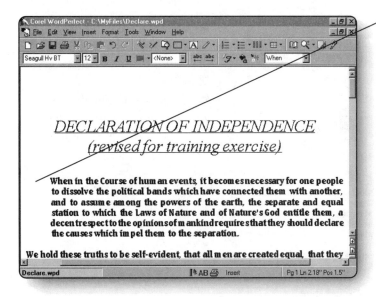

The paragraph will be indented per your selection.

CENTERING A PAGE VERTICALLY

Aesthetically, title pages look better when centered vertically. You may even want to vertically center the first page of a letter.

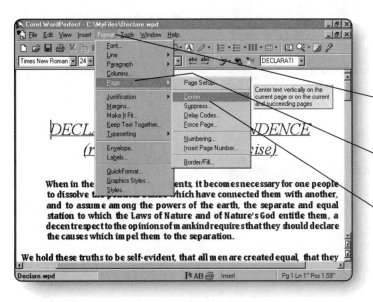

1. **Position** the **insertion point** on the page to be centered vertically.

2. **Click** on **Format**. The Format menu will appear.

3. **Click** on **Page**. The Page cascading menu will appear.

4. **Click** on **Center**. The Center Page(s) dialog box will open.

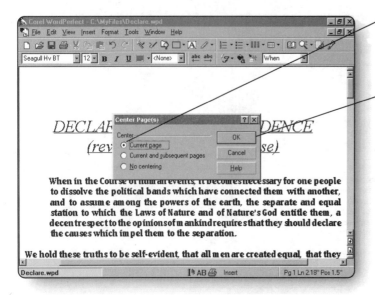

5. Click on **Current Page** or **Current and Subsequent Pages**, depending on your needs.

6. Click on **OK**. The dialog box will close and the page will be centered vertically from the top to bottom margin.

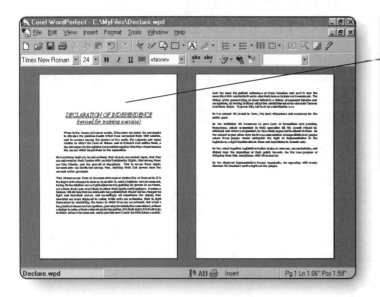

TIP

The best way to see a page that been centered vertically is to use Two Page view or Full Page view. Views are covered in Chapter 5.

CHANGING LINE SPACING

Line spacing changes the distance between lines of text from the position of your insertion point downward in your document. The default choice in WordPerfect is single spacing.

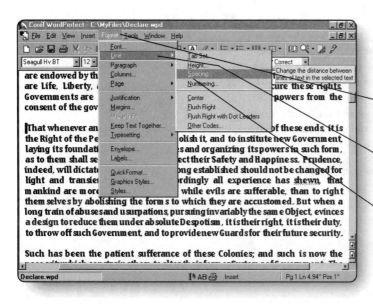

1. Position the **insertion point** where you want the line spacing change to begin.

2. Click on **Format**. The Format menu will appear.

3. Click on **Line**. The Line cascading menu will appear.

4. Click on **Spacing**. The Line Spacing dialog box will open.

TIP

If you only want a section of the document to have the new line spacing, highlight that section first.

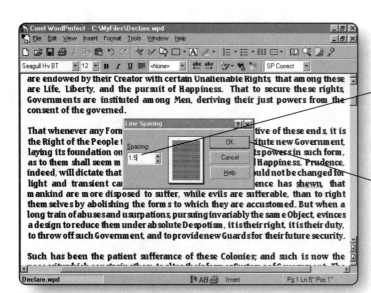

5. Type the **desired spacing** in the Spacing: box. Type 2 for double spacing, 1.5 for one and one-half line spacing, and so on.

6. Click on **OK**. The dialog box will close.

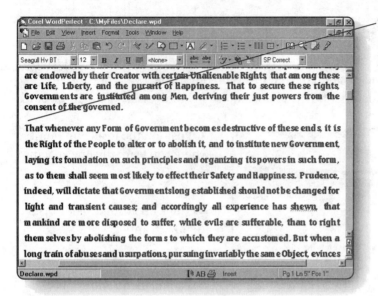

The document from the insertion point downward will have the new line spacing.

10 Adding Bullets, Numbering, and Borders

Bullets and borders call attention to points in a document. Numbered lists allow the reader to follow steps in a sequential order. In this chapter, you'll learn how to:

- ✦ Add a bullet
- ✦ Create a numbered list
- ✦ Add a border to a paragraph
- ✦ Add a fill color to a paragraph
- ✦ Put a border around a page

ADDING A BULLET

Bullets call attention to a list of items. They come in several styles, so you can use different kinds of lists or suit the bullets to your subject.

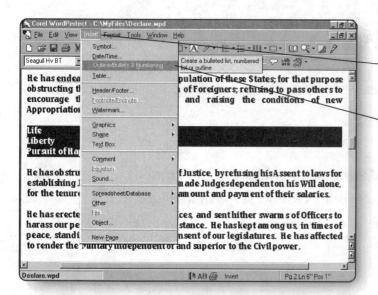

1. Select the **text** to be bulleted.

2. Click on **Insert**. The Insert menu will appear.

3. Click on **Outline/Bullets and Numbering**. The Bullets and Numbering dialog box will open.

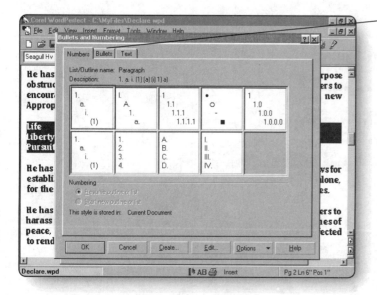

4. Click on the **Bullets tab**. The tab will come to the top of the stack.

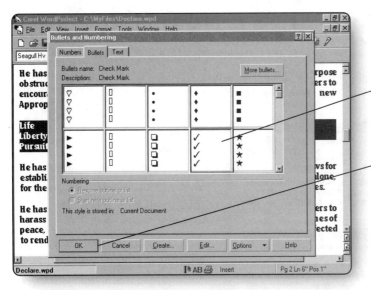

There are 10 different styles of bullets ranging from small solid circles to stars.

5. **Click** on the desired **bullet style**. A dark border will appear around your selection.

6. **Click** on **OK**. The dialog box will close.

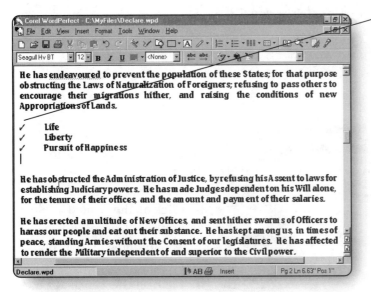

The selected text will be indented and have bullets in front of each paragraph.

TIP

If you click the mouse at the end of a bulleted item and then press the Enter key, the next item you type will have a bullet as well.

CREATING A NUMBERED LIST

Numbered lists are frequently used to list steps of a project. The sequencing makes reading easier. There are nine different styles of numbering, including Roman numerals.

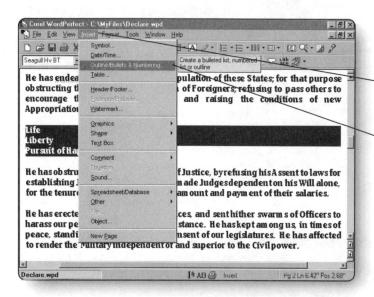

1. **Select** the **text** to be numbered.

2. **Click** on **Insert**. The Insert menu will appear.

3. **Click** on **Outline/Bullets and Numbering**. The Bullets and Numbering dialog box will open.

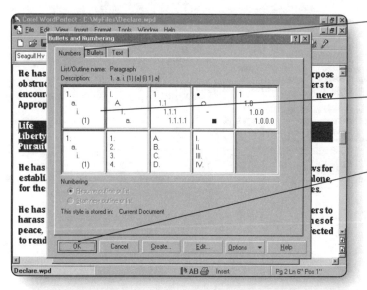

4. **Click** on the **Numbers tab.** The tab will come to the top of the stack.

5. **Click** on the desired **description**. A dark border will appear around your selection.

6. **Click** on **OK**. The dialog box will close.

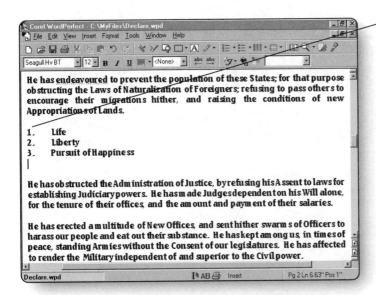

The selected text will be indented and numbered.

ADDING A BORDER TO A PARAGRAPH

Another way to call attention to specific text is to put a border around it.

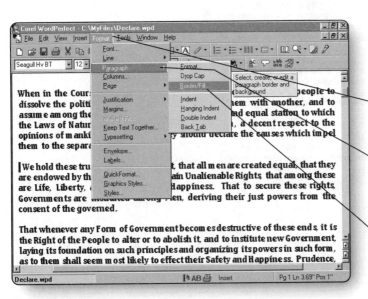

1. **Position** the **insertion point** in the paragraph to have a border.

2. **Click** on **Format**. The Format menu will appear.

3. **Click** on **Paragraph**. The Paragraph cascading menu will appear.

4. **Click** on **Border/Fill**. The Paragraph Border/Fill dialog box will open.

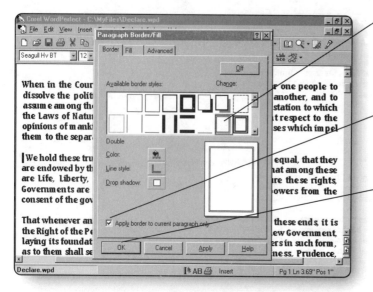

5. **Click** on a **style** from the Available border styles: box. A dark line will appear around your selection.

6. **Click** on **Apply border to current paragraph only**. A ✔ will appear in the check box.

7. **Click** on **OK**. The dialog box will close.

The paragraph will have a border around it.

When in the Course of human events, it becomes necessary for one people to dissolve the political bands which have connected them with another, and to assume among the powers of the earth, the separate and equal station to which the Laws of Nature and of Nature's God entitle them, a decent respect to the opinions of mankind requires that they should declare the causes which impel them to the separation.

We hold these truths to be self-evident, that all men are created equal, that they are endowed by their Creator with certain Unalienable Rights, that among these are Life, Liberty, and the pursuit of Happiness. That to secure these rights, Governments are instituted among Men, deriving their just powers from the consent of the governed.

That whenever any Form of Government becomes destructive of these ends, it is the Right of the People to alter or to abolish it, and to institute new Government, laying its foundation on such principles and organizing its powers in such form,

ADDING A FILL COLOR TO A PARAGRAPH

Adding fill color to a paragraph puts the text on a different background from the rest of the page.

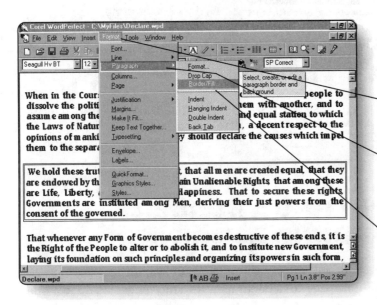

1. **Position** the **insertion point** in the paragraph to have a filled background.

2. **Click** on **Format**. The Format menu will appear.

3. **Click** on **Paragraph**. The Paragraph cascading menu will appear.

4. **Click** on **Border/Fill**. The Paragraph Border/Fill dialog box will open.

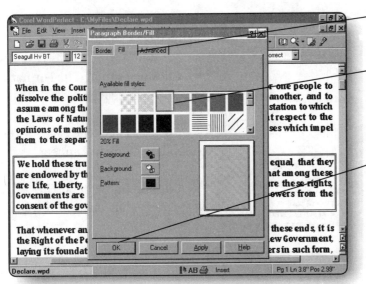

5. **Click** on the **Fill tab**. The tab will come to the top of the stack.

6. **Click** on a **style** from the Available fill styles: scroll box. A dark line will appear around your selection.

7. **Click** on **OK**. The dialog box will close.

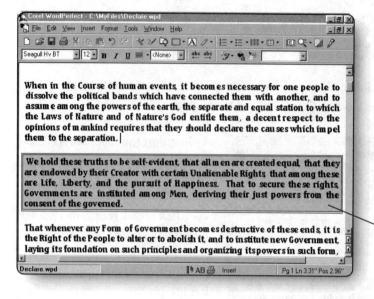

TIP

Keep the fill color light and solid if your text is to be black; otherwise you won't be able to read the text. If you do want a dark background, for example, 100% black, change the text color to white.

The paragraph will have a filled background.

PUTTING A BORDER AROUND A PAGE

Page Borders will put a border around a entire page or multiple pages of a document. It's a nice effect to add to a title page of a report.

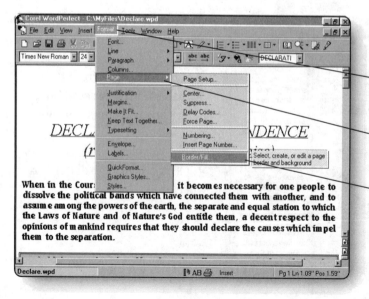

1. **Position** the **insertion point** in the page to have a border.

2. **Click** on **Format**. The Format menu will appear.

3. **Click** on **Page**. The Page cascading menu will appear.

4. **Click** on **Border/Fill**. The Page Border/Fill dialog box will open.

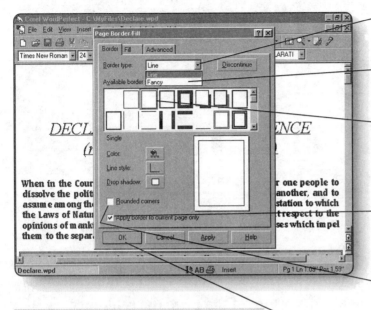

5. **Click** on the **down arrow (▼)** next to the Border type: list box.

6. **Click** on **Fancy** or **Line** for the type of border.

7. **Click** on a **style** from the Available border styles: scroll box. A dark line will appear around your selection.

8. **Click** on **Apply border to current page only.** A ✔ will appear in the check box.

9. Optionally, **click** on **Rounded Corners** to give the border curved edges.

NOTE

Steps 8 and 9 are only available when you choose Line for the Border type.

10. **Click** on **OK.** The dialog box will close.

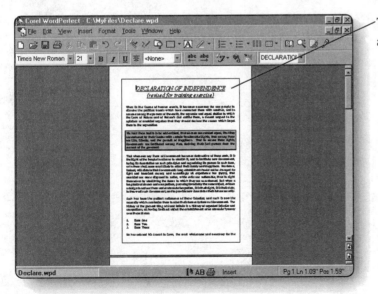

The page will have a border around it.

11 Working with Footnotes and Endnotes

Giving credit where credit is due is what footnotes and endnotes are all about. Footnotes are at the bottom of the page the reference is on and endnotes are traditionally at the end of the report. In this chapter, you'll learn how to:

✦ Create and edit a footnote or endnote

✦ Move and delete a footnote or endnote

✦ Change a footnote to an endnote

CREATING FOOTNOTES AND ENDNOTES

It will be easier to work on footnotes or endnotes if you are in Page view.

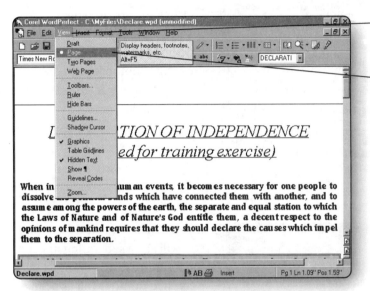

1. **Click** on **View**. The View menu will appear.

2. **Click** on **Page**. The view will switch to Page view.

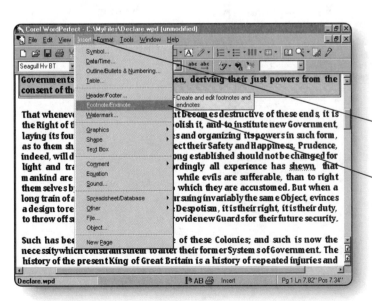

3. **Position** the **insertion point** at the location where the footnote reference number should appear.

4. **Click** on **Insert**. The Insert menu will appear.

5. **Click** on **Footnote/Endnote**. The Footnote/Endnote dialog box will open.

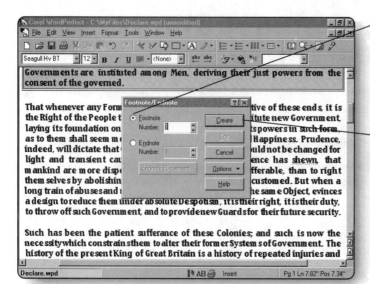

6. **Click** on the **option button** next to Footnote Number or Endnote Number. WordPerfect will automatically number the footnotes and endnotes for you.

7. **Click** on **Create**. The insertion point will jump to the bottom of the screen if you are creating a footnote or to the end of the document if you are creating an endnote.

If you chose to make a footnote, you will see a separating line for the footnote text, and the reference number will appear. For either footnotes or endnotes, the reference is automatically numbered and superscripted for you.

8. **Type** the **footnote** or **endnote text**.

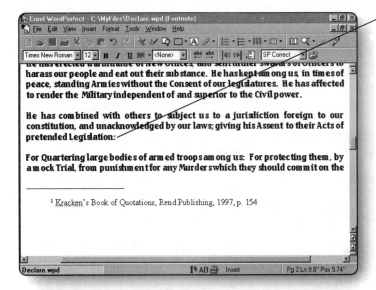

9. **Click anywhere** above the footnote separator line or the endnote reference number to leave the note text area and return to your document.

The reference number also appears in the body of your document.

NOTE

If you are not in Page view you will not be able to see the footnote text at the bottom of the page.

EDITING FOOTNOTES AND ENDNOTES

Editing a footnote or endnote is like editing any other text in a WordPerfect document.

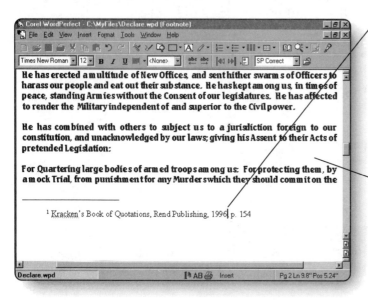

1. **Position** the **insertion point** in the footnote text at the bottom of the page or in the endnote text at the bottom of the document.

2. **Type** any necessary **corrections** or **changes**.

3. **Click anywhere** in the body of your document to resume editing.

MOVING FOOTNOTES AND ENDNOTES

If you move text that contains a footnote or endnote, WordPerfect will change the reference number automatically, if necessary.

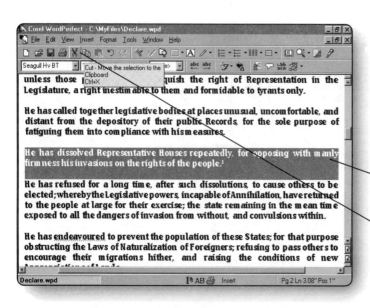

1. **Select** the **text** to be moved, including the reference number.

2. **Click** on the **Cut button**. The text including the footnote reference information will be placed on the Clipboard.

3. **Position** the **insertion point** where the text is to be placed.

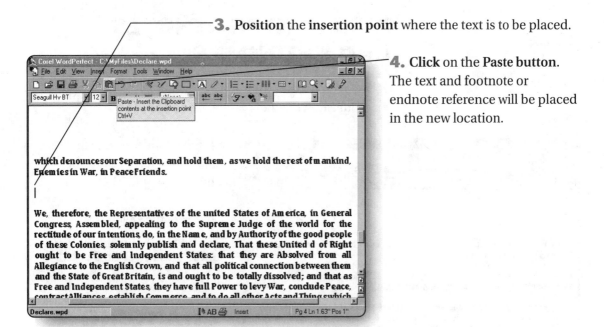

4. **Click** on the **Paste button.** The text and footnote or endnote reference will be placed in the new location.

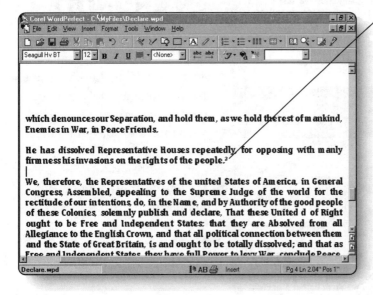

If necessary, WordPerfect will renumber the footnote.

DELETING FOOTNOTES AND ENDNOTES

Deleting a footnote or endnote is as easy as deleting regular text from a document.

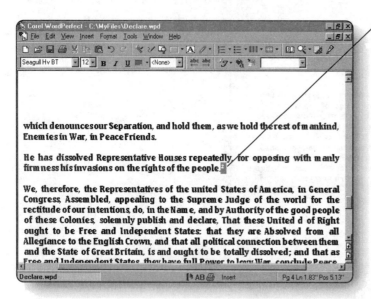

1. Select the **footnote** or **endnote reference number** in the body of your document.

2. Press the **Delete key**. The reference and the footnote or endnote text will be deleted.

CHANGING A FOOTNOTE TO AN ENDNOTE

If you need to change your footnotes to endnotes (or vice versa), you do not have to delete the footnotes and retype them as endnotes. WordPerfect gives you a macro to convert them for you.

1. Click on **Tools**. The Tools menu will appear.

2. Click on **Macro**. The Macro cascading menu will appear.

3. Click on **Play**. The Play Macro dialog box will open.

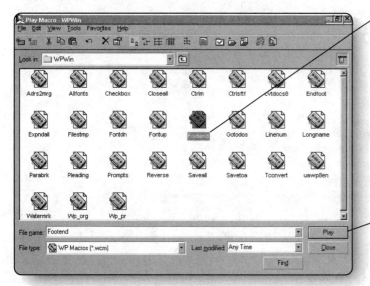

4. **Click** on **Footend**. This is the macro to convert footnotes to endnotes.

5. **Click** on **Play**. The macro will execute and all footnotes will be changed to endnotes.

12

Adding Headers, Footers, and Watermarks

One of the time-saving features of WordPerfect is the ability to add a header or footer. You only need create the header or footer information one time and WordPerfect will insert it at the top or bottom of each page of your document. Watermarks will allow you to insert text or graphics underneath the body of your document, creating an almost subliminal effect. In this chapter, you'll learn how to:

✦ Add a header or footer

✦ Insert the path and filename

✦ Edit a header or footer

✦ Suppress a header or footer

✦ Discontinue a header or footer

✦ Add a watermark

ADDING A HEADER OR FOOTER

If you have text or graphics you want to appear at the top or bottom of each page, you can add a header or footer. A header will appear at the top of every page and a footer at the bottom of every page.

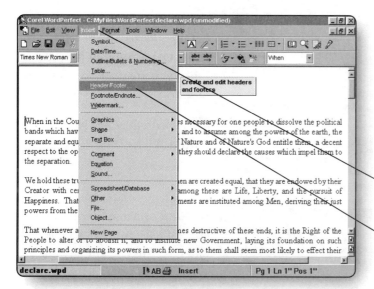

1. **Position** the **insertion point** on the page where you want the header or footer to begin. For example, position it at the top of the document.

2. **Click** on **Insert**. The Insert menu will appear.

3. **Click** on **Header/Footer**. The Headers/Footers dialog box will open.

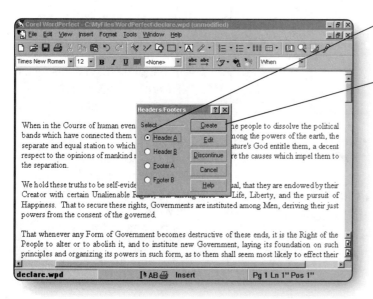

4. **Click** on **Header A** or **Footer A**, whichever you want to insert.

5. **Click** on **Create**. Your insertion point will jump to the top or bottom margin of the page.

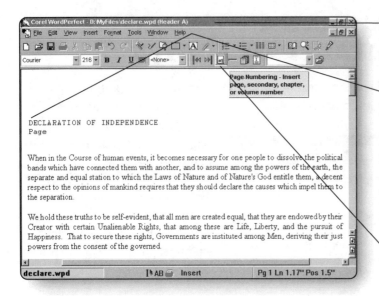

Notice the Title Bar of the window reflects you are in the header (or footer) area.

6. **Type** the **text** desired for the header or footer.

Do not type a page number here. Let WordPerfect fill in the correct page number for you. When you are ready for the page number:

7. **Click** on the **Page Numbering button**. A list of choices will appear.

8. **Click** on **Page Number**. The current page number will be entered. This is really a code to WordPerfect and will update as the pages change.

9. **Click anywhere** in your document outside the header/footer area to exit the header or footer.

TIP

If you want to enter the total number of pages such as Page x of y, where x is the current page number and y is the total number of pages: type the word *Page* and a space; click on the Page Number button and choose Page Number; type a space, the word *of,* and then another space; finally, click on the Page Number button and choose Total Pages.

INSERTING THE PATH AND FILENAME

Oftentimes you want to insert the filename and location of a document. You can put it in the header or footer, or in the body text of the document. To use this feature, you must have first saved the document and given it a name.

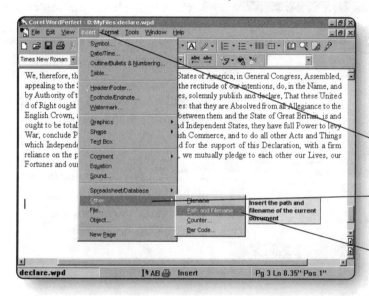

1. Position the **insertion point** where you want the location and filename to be located.

2. Click on **Insert**. The Insert menu will appear.

3. Click on **Other**. The Other cascading menu will appear.

4. Click on **Path and Filename**.

The document path and filename will be placed at the insertion point.

NOTE

The path and filename are *dynamic,* which means that if you move the document to another folder or give it a different name, the change will be reflected in the document.

EDITING A HEADER OR FOOTER

Editing a header or footer is quite easy as long as you are in Page view.

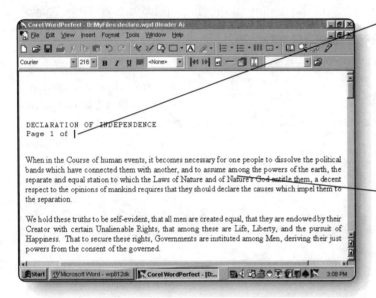

1. **Click** in the **header** or **footer area** on the screen. Notice the Title Bar at the top reflects that you are in the header or footer.

2. **Make** any desired **changes or corrections** to the header or footer text.

3. **Click anywhere** in the body of the document. You are now able to return to editing the body of your document.

SUPPRESSING A HEADER OR FOOTER

Occasionally there is a page that you do not want the header, footer, page numbering, or watermark to print on. It could be the first page of a letter or report, or it could be any page in the middle of the report. WordPerfect will allow you to suppress the printing for a specific page.

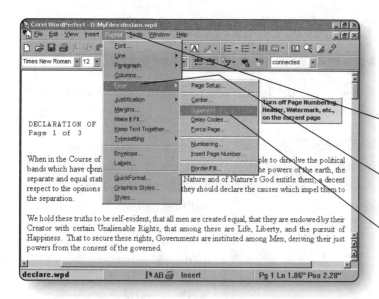

1. **Position** the **insertion point** on the page where you do not want the header or footer to print.

2. **Click** on **Format**. The Format menu will appear.

3. **Click** on **Page**. The Page cascading menu will appear.

4. **Click** on **Suppress**. The Suppress dialog box will open.

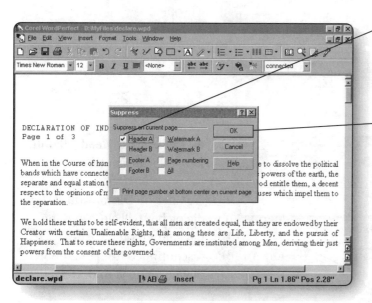

5. **Click** on the **items** you do not want to print. A ✔ will be placed in the check box beside each item you click.

6. **Click** on **OK**. The dialog box will close.

NOTE

Suppress will only suppress information on the current page.

DISCONTINUING A HEADER OR FOOTER

If you wish to stop the printing of a header or footer you can discontinue it.

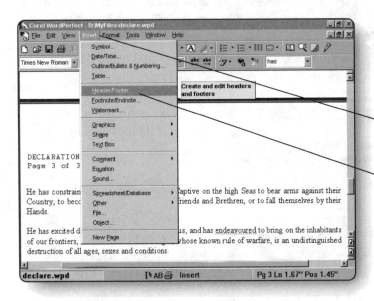

1. **Place** the **insertion point** on the page where you want the header or footer to discontinue printing.

2. **Click** on **Insert**. The Insert menu will appear.

3. **Click** on **Header/Footer**. The Headers/Footers dialog box will open.

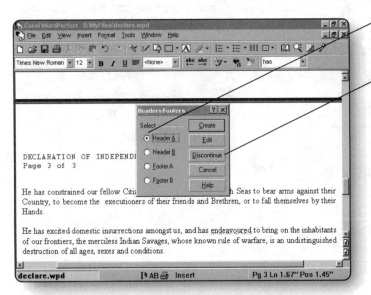

4. **Click** on the **Header/Footer item** to be discontinued.

5. **Click** on **Discontinue**. The dialog box will close and the header or footer will be discontinued from that point downward in your document.

ADDING A WATERMARK

You can print a watermark (background image) behind the text on a page. You can use clip art images, an existing file, or text for a watermark. You can also adjust the shading (or lightness) of a watermark. A watermark is like a header or footer in that it will begin on a specified page and continue through each page of your document unless you suppress or discontinue it.

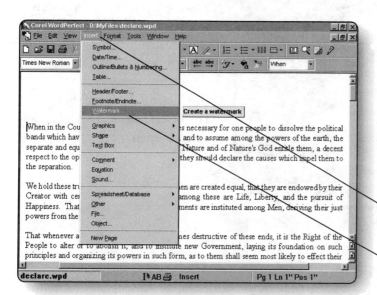

1. **Position** the **insertion point** on the page where you would like the watermark to begin appearing.

2. **Click** on **Insert**. The Insert menu will appear.

3. **Click** on **Watermark**. The Watermark dialog box will open.

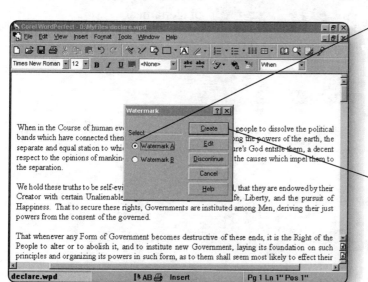

4. **Click** on **Watermark A**. By default, the watermark will appear on every page, however, you can have two different watermarks; one on the odd-numbered pages, and the other on the even-numbered pages.

5. **Click** on **Create**.

Don't panic! You did not lose your text. Look at the top of your window. The Title Bar at the top shows that you are in the watermark area.

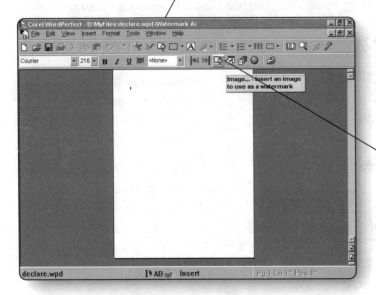

What you are seeing is the background of your document. It is displayed in Full Page view. You are now ready to add a graphic image to the background of your document.

6. **Click** on the **Image button**. The Insert Image - ClipArt dialog box will open.

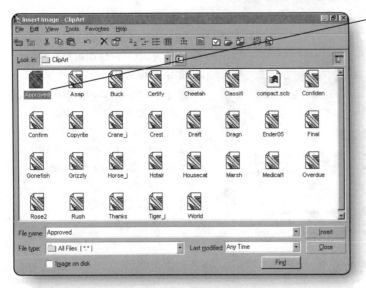

7. **Select** a **graphic** from the list of filenames.

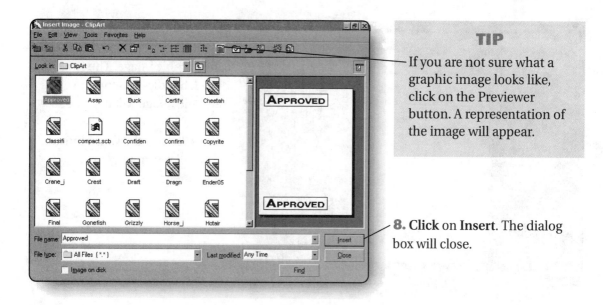

8. Click on **Insert**. The dialog box will close.

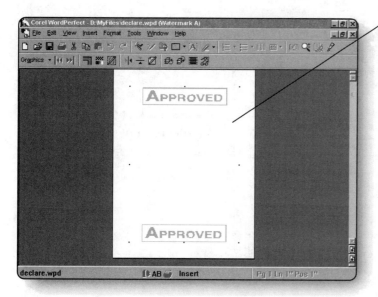

The graphic image appears on the background page in a light gray shading with eight small black dots called *handles* around it.

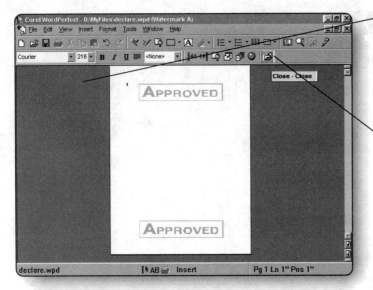

9. Click in the **gray area** outside the background page to deselect the graphic image. The small black handles around the graphic image will disappear.

10. Click on the **Close button**. You will return to your document.

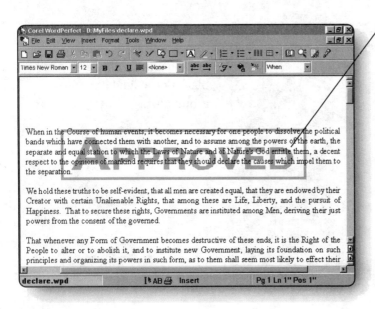

The image appears underneath the text of your document.

NOTE
Watermarks, headers, and footers do not show on your screen if you are in Draft view.

13 Saving Time with Templates

WordPerfect has included some great time-saving templates for you—sample documents with all sorts of special formatting. WordPerfect has done most of the work for you and has a feature called PerfectExpert to guide you in using them. In this chapter, you'll learn how to:

✦ **Create a memo**

✦ **Create an award certificate**

✦ **Create a greeting card**

CREATING A MEMO

This template contains several predesigned looks for your memos. Try them all out to find your favorite!

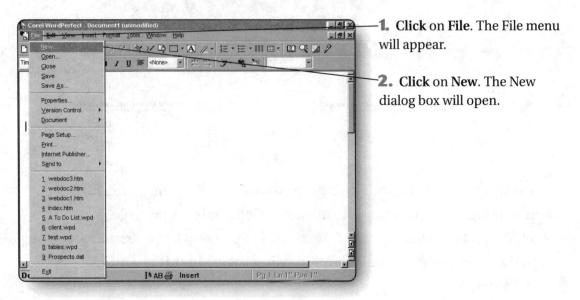

1. **Click** on **File**. The File menu will appear.

2. **Click** on **New**. The New dialog box will open.

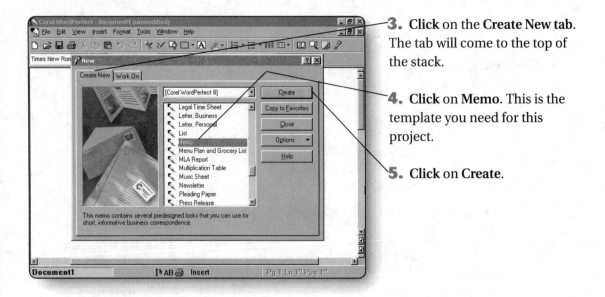

3. **Click** on the **Create New tab**. The tab will come to the top of the stack.

4. **Click** on **Memo**. This is the template you need for this project.

5. **Click** on **Create**.

The PerfectExpert will appear on the left side.

A blank document will appear on the right side.

Then, a Memo Expert dialog box will open, prompting you for information regarding the memo.

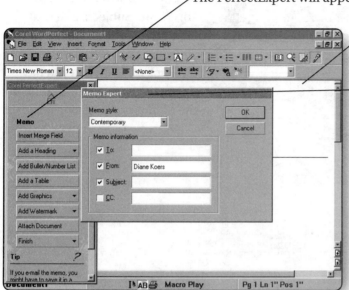

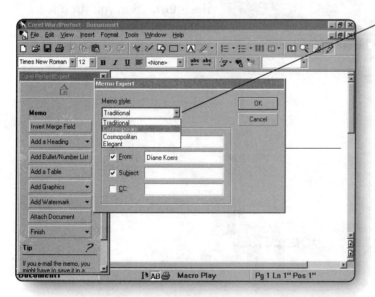

6. Click on a **memo style**: Traditional, Contemporary, Cosmopolitan, or Elegant.

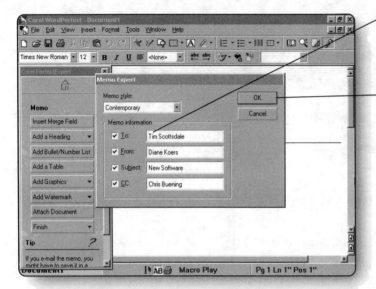

7. Enter information in the To:, From:, Subject:, and CC: text boxes.

8. Click on **OK** when you have finished entering information in the Memo Expert dialog box.

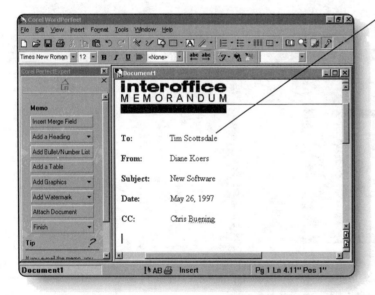

The Memo Expert will close and the information you supplied will be placed in the document at the appropriate location.

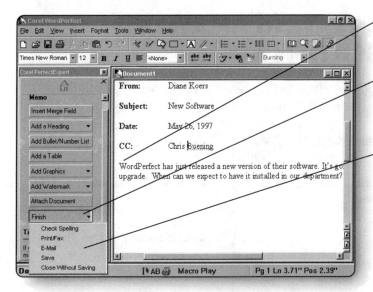

9. **Finish typing** the body of the memo.

10. **Click** on the **Finish button** on the PerfectExpert window. A list of choices will appear.

11. **Click** on any **steps** you want WordPerfect to take next: Check the spelling in the memo, print or fax the memo, e-mail the memo, save the memo (closing it at the same time), or close the memo without saving it.

12. **Click** on the **Close button**. The PerfectExpert dialog box will close.

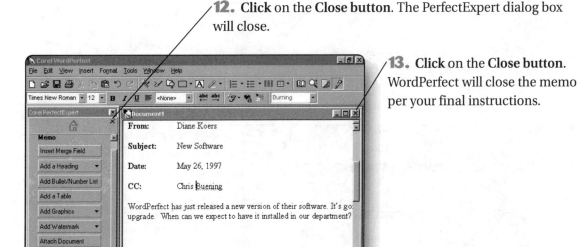

13. **Click** on the **Close button**. WordPerfect will close the memo per your final instructions.

CREATING AN AWARD CERTIFICATE

Another template that can save you time is the Award certificate. Tell someone how much you appreciate their hard work without any hard work on your part!

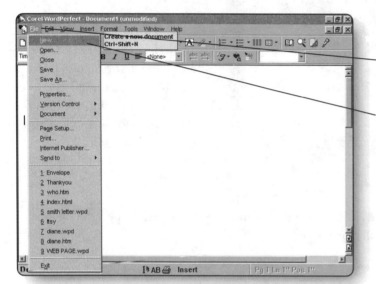

1. **Click** on **File**. The File menu will appear.

2. **Click** on **New**. The New dialog box will open.

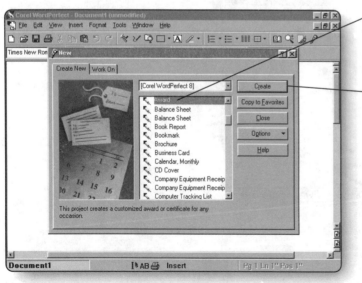

3. **Click** on **Award**. This is the template to help you create a certificate.

4. **Click** on **Create**.

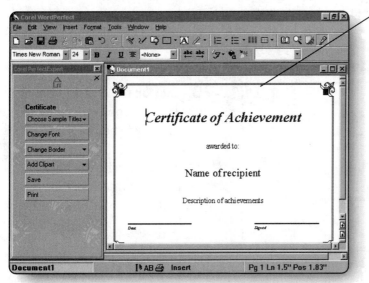

A Certificate of Achievement will appear in Full Page view as well as the PerfectExpert to help you make any changes.

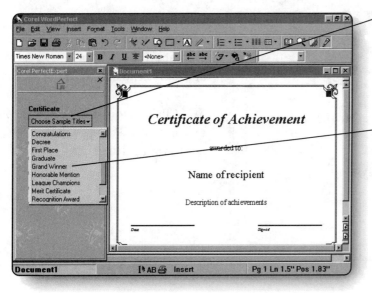

5. **Click** on the **Choose Sample Titles button** to change the certificate type. Be sure to scroll down the list to look at all 23 possible titles.

6. **Click** on an appropriate **title** for your certificate. The title of the certificate will automatically change for you.

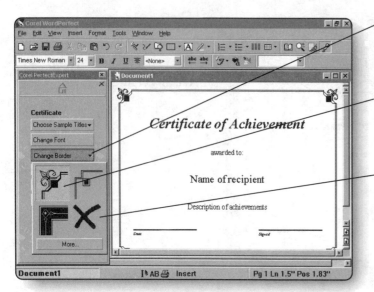

7. Click on the **Change Border button** to see available border styles.

8. Click on the desired **style** of **border**. The border around the certificate will be changed.

The selection with the big X means "no border" on the certificate.

9. Click on the **Add Clipart button** to view a few selected graphics that might be appropriate to an award.

10. Click on the desired **graphic**. WordPerfect will insert it into your certificate.

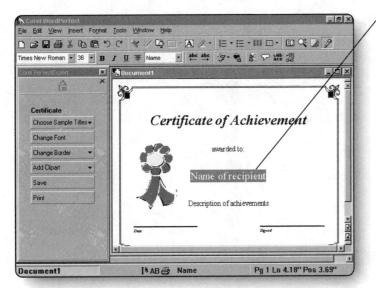

11. Select "Name of recipient" and **type** in its place the award **recipient's name**.

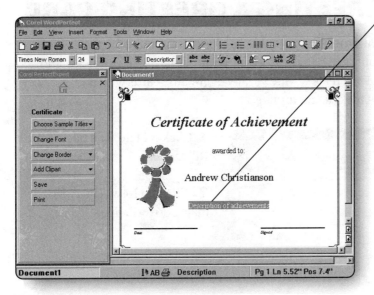

12. **Select** the words **"Description of achievements"** and **replace** them with an actual **description** of the award.

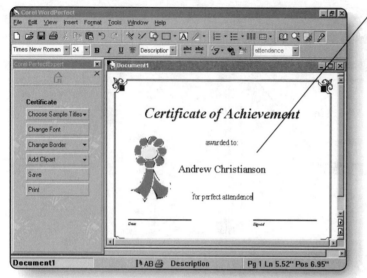

Your certificate is now complete and can be printed and/or saved.

CREATING A GREETING CARD

With the advent of today's nice color printers, why not create your own personalized greeting cards? You can quickly and easily create a wide variety of greeting cards with a WordPerfect template.

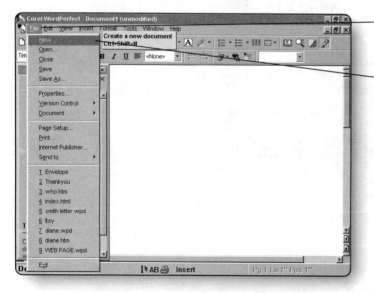

1. **Click** on **File**. The File menu will appear.

2. **Click** on **New**. The New dialog box will open.

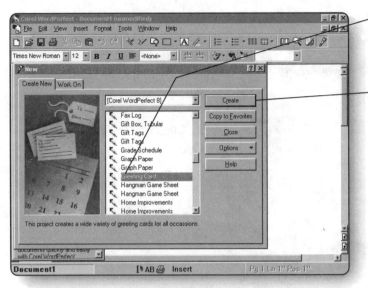

3. Click on **Greeting Card**. This is the template to help you design a greeting card.

4. Click on **Create**.

A sample greeting card will appear as well as the PerfectExpert to help you personalize your card.

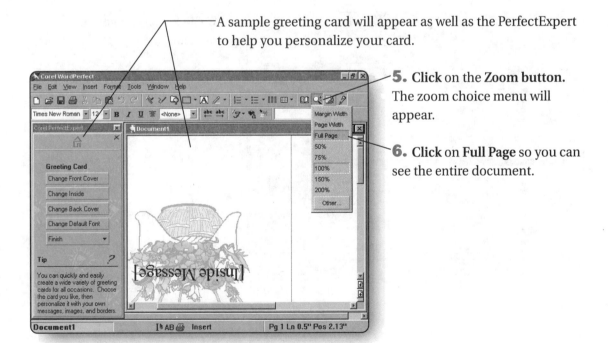

5. Click on the **Zoom button.** The zoom choice menu will appear.

6. Click on **Full Page** so you can see the entire document.

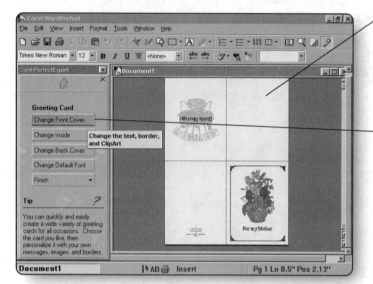

Notice how the card has been divided into four sections. When completed, you can fold the card into the four sections to make your greeting card.

7. **Click** on the **Change Front Cover button** to choose a different style of card.

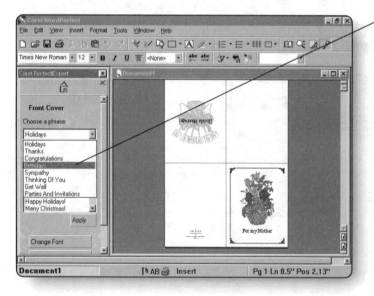

8. **Click** on a **category** for your card.

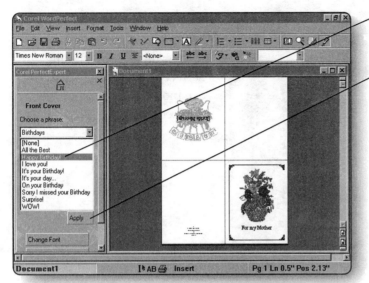

9. Click on the appropriate **phrase** for the front of your card.

10. Click on **Apply**. The front cover of the greeting card will change.

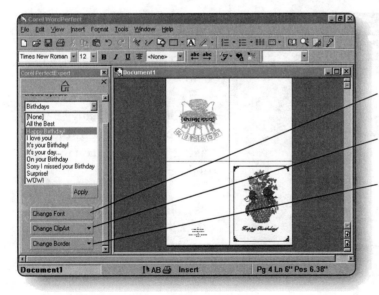

Other options available to modify for the front of your card include:

+ Change Font to select a different font.

+ Change ClipArt to choose a different piece of artwork.

+ Change Border to pick a different style of border.

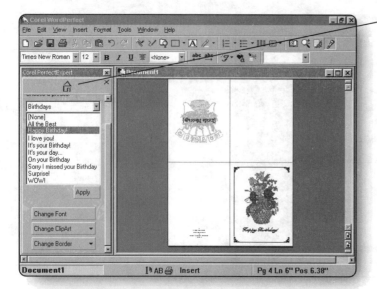

11. Click on the **PerfectExpert's Project Home button**. This will return you to the beginning PerfectExpert screen where you can modify other elements of the greeting card.

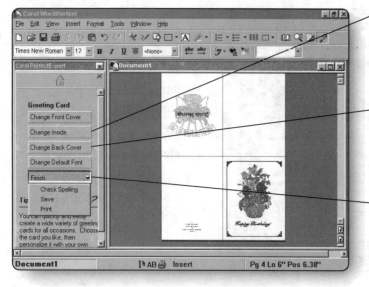

12. Click on the **Change Inside button** to change the message or clip art on the inside area of the card.

13. Click on the **Change Back Cover button** to modify the credits to be printed on the back of the card.

14. Click on the **Finish button** to spell check, save, or print your greeting card.

PART II REVIEW QUESTIONS

1. What is the default font for a WordPerfect document? *See "Changing the Typeface" in Chapter 7*

2. Approximately how tall is a 72-point font? *See "Changing Font Size" in Chapter 7*

3. Which view does page numbering not appear in? *See "Adding Page Numbering" in Chapter 8*

4. Why should you select text first before choosing to center a heading? *See "Centering a Heading" in Chapter 9*

5. What is the difference between an Indent and a Double Indent? *See "Indenting a Paragraph" in Chapter 9*

6. How many styles of bullets does WordPerfect show you? *See "Adding a Bullet" in Chapter 10*

7. Which feature shows a separating line at the bottom of a page—a footnote or an endnote? *See "Creating Footnotes and Endnotes" in Chapter 11*

8. What is the name of the macro that converts a footnote to and endnote? *See "Changing a Footnote to an Endnote" in Chapter 11*

9. How many pages does suppress affect? *See "Suppressing a Header or Footer" in Chapter 12*

10. Can you add clip art to an award certificate created with a WordPerfect template? *See "Creating an Award Certificate" in Chapter 13*

PART III

Working with Tables

14 Creating a Table Using Tabs

WordPerfect has built-in default tab settings and it will also allow you to create your own settings. There are four styles of tab settings and each of those can have dot leaders in front of them, if desired. In this chapter, you'll learn how to:

✦ Turn on the Ruler Bar

✦ Work with the default tabs

✦ Add a custom tab stop

✦ Delete a tab stop

TURNING ON THE RULER BAR

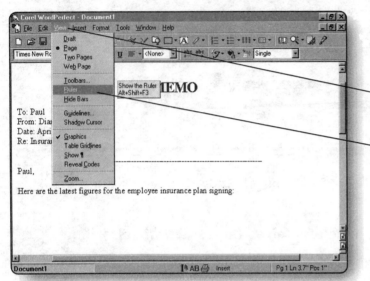

If you are going to be modifying tabs, it is extremely helpful to turn on the Ruler Bar.

1. **Click** on **View**. The View menu will appear.

2. **Click** on **Ruler**.

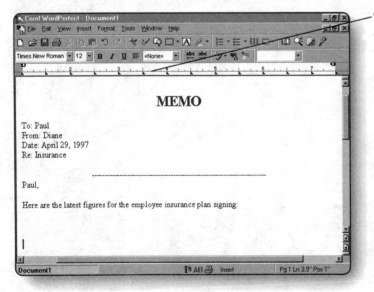

The Ruler Bar will appear with the current tab settings.

CHANGING THE DEFAULT TABS

By default, WordPerfect assigns left-aligned tabs at half-inch intervals. If you would like to change that, for example, to quarter-inch intervals, use the Tab Set dialog box.

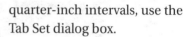
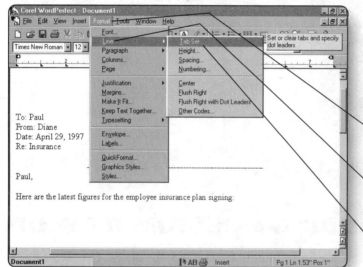

1. **Position** the **insertion point** where you would like the new tab settings to go into effect.

2. **Click** on **Format**. The Format menu will appear.

3. **Click** on **Line**. The Line cascading menu will appear.

4. **Click** on **Tab Set**. The Tab Set dialog box will open.

5. **Click** on **Repeat Every**. A ✔ will appear in the check box and the measurement box to the right will now be available.

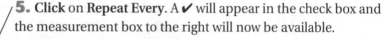

6. **Select** the **default measurement** (0.50").

7. **Type** the **desired increment** in a decimal format. You could type it 0.25, .25, or .25". Whether you add the zero in front of the decimal point or whether you add the inch mark (") doesn't matter to WordPerfect. It will automatically put them in for you.

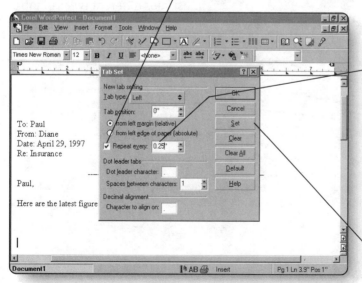

8. **Click** on the **Set button**. The new setting will go into effect.

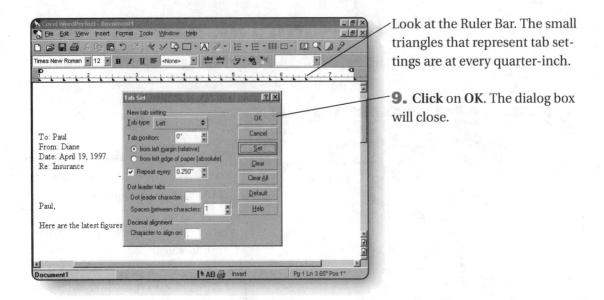

Look at the Ruler Bar. The small triangles that represent tab settings are at every quarter-inch.

9. Click on **OK**. The dialog box will close.

ADDING A CUSTOM TAB STOP

There are four different types of tabs available: left-aligned, right-aligned, center-aligned, and decimal-aligned. Tabs can have dot leaders added to keep the eye focused on a particular line of the document. You can create a custom tab setting using any combination of these tabs. The following figure illustrates different types of tabs:

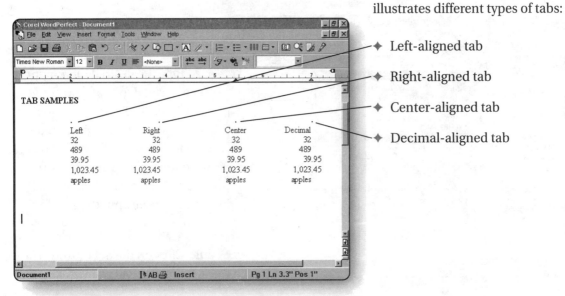

+ Left-aligned tab

+ Right-aligned tab

+ Center-aligned tab

+ Decimal-aligned tab

1. **Position** the **insertion point** where you would like the new tab settings to take effect.

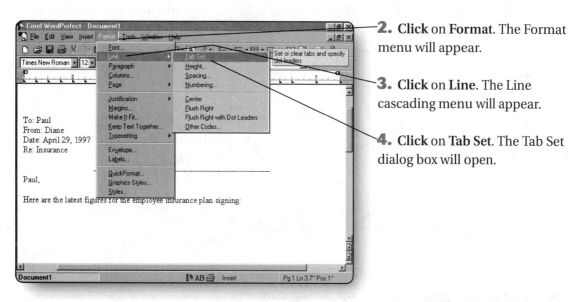

2. **Click** on **Format**. The Format menu will appear.

3. **Click** on **Line**. The Line cascading menu will appear.

4. **Click** on **Tab Set**. The Tab Set dialog box will open.

5. **Click** on the **Clear All button**. All existing tabs will be deleted.

6. **Click** on **OK**. The Tab Set dialog box will close.

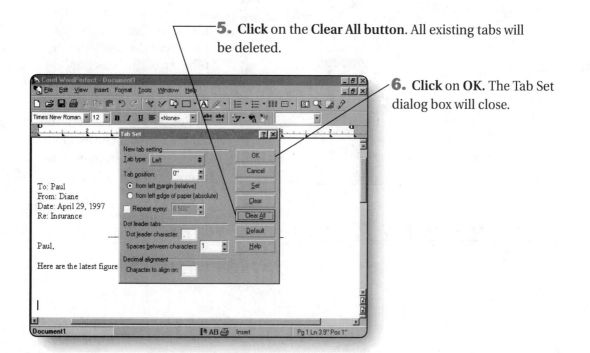

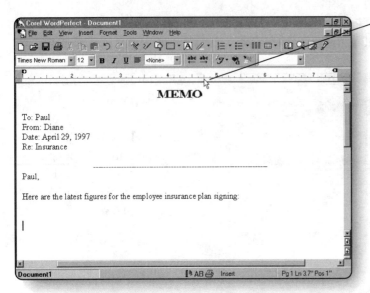

7. Position the **mouse pointer** on the tab area of the ruler line. Be sure you are in the tab area, which is directly below the bottom of the ruler line. The mouse pointer will turn into a white arrow.

8. Click on the **right mouse button**. The tab shortcut menu will appear.

NOTE

Make sure the menu you see is like the one in this figure. If not, try again. You may not have been exactly in the tab area of the ruler line.

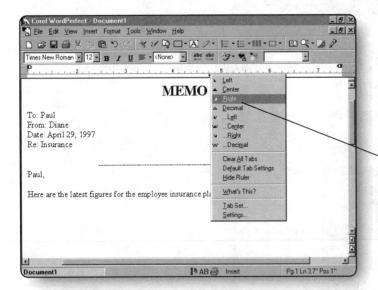

9. Click on the **style of tab** you would like to use. The first four will have no dot leader in front of them, but the next four choices will have a dot leader. The menu will close when you have made a selection.

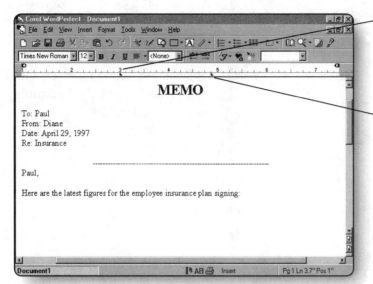

10. Click on the **tab area** of the Ruler Bar wherever you want the new tab setting to appear. A small triangle will appear.

11. Repeat steps 6 through **8** for each additional tab stop you wish to place.

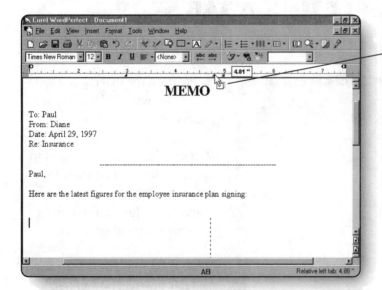

TIP

To move a tab stop, position the mouse pointer on top of the tab stop. The mouse pointer will turn into a rectangular box with the mouse pointer on top of it. Drag the tab stop to the new position.

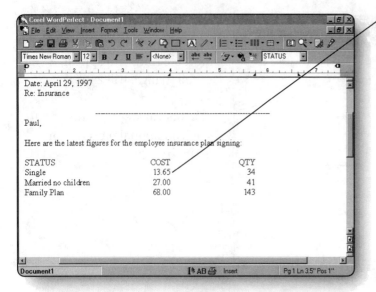

You are now ready to begin typing text into your document, pressing the Tab key whenever you want to jump to the next tab stop. Look how neatly the figures line up in this table!

DELETING A TAB STOP

Deleting an unwanted tab stop is easy in WordPerfect!

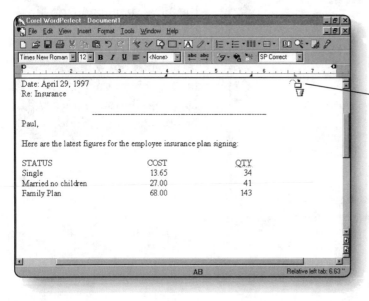

1. **Position** the **insertion point** where you would like the new tab settings to take effect.

2. **Drag** the **unwanted tab stop** off the Ruler Bar into the white part of the WordPerfect document. The mouse pointer turns into a small trash can.

3. **Release** the **mouse button**. The tab stop will be deleted.

15 Creating a WordPerfect Table

WordPerfect tables are like small spreadsheets built right into your documents. Tables have formulas and functions just like your spreadsheet program. If you have already created a file with your spreadsheet program, you can even insert it into your WordPerfect document. In this chapter, you'll learn how to:

✦ Insert a table in the document

✦ Enter information in a table

✦ Save time with QuickFill

✦ Add a row at the beginning and end of a table

✦ Add a column to a table

✦ Delete a row or column

✦ Insert an existing spreadsheet into a document

INSERTING A TABLE IN A DOCUMENT

The maximum table size is 64 columns by 32,767 rows. That ought to be big enough!

1. **Position** the **insertion point** at the location where you want the table to appear.

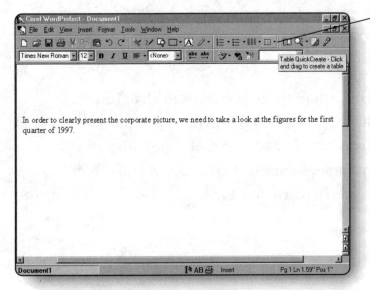

2. **Press** and **hold** the **Table QuickCreate button**. A small grid will open. This grid represents the columns and rows of a table.

TIP

If you plan on placing the table at the beginning of your document, press the Enter key once before you create the table. This will give you a small space at the top in the event you decide to add something ahead of the table. If you decide not to keep that space, you can always delete it later.

NOTE

The maximum number of columns that can be added with this method is 32. If you need more than 32 columns, you must use the Insert menu and click on Table. From there you can create a table with up to 64 columns.

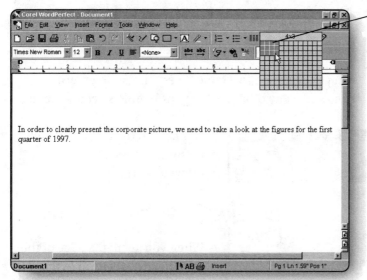

3. **Drag** the **mouse pointer** over the squares of the grid until you have covered enough to represent the size of your table.

As you are dragging across the grid, notice the numbers at the top. These represent how many columns and rows you have selected. For example, 4 x 3 will give you a table with four columns and three rows.

4. **Release** the **mouse button**. A table will be inserted into your document.

Notice the Property Bar has changed. It now contains buttons for working with tables.

ENTERING INFORMATION IN A TABLE

Entering information in a table is very similar to entering information in any other part of your WordPerfect document.

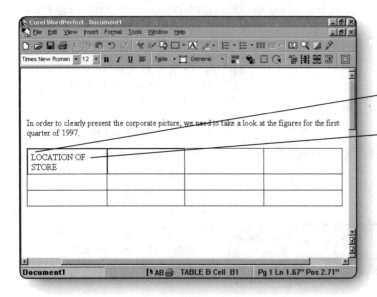

1. **Position** the **insertion point** in the cell to receive information.

2. **Type text.**

When you get to the edge of the cell, the text will wrap to the next line of that cell.

NOTE

If you don't want the text to wrap to the next line of the cell, let it wrap anyway. In Chapter 16, you will discover how to change the width of cells as well as how to join cells together.

3. **Press** the **Tab key**. The insertion point will move to the next cell.

TIP

Press and hold the Shift key while pressing the Tab key to move to a previous cell.

SAVING TIME WITH QUICKFILL

Use QuickFill to continue a pattern of values across a row or down a column. You can use days of the week, months, quarters, numbers, or Roman numerals.

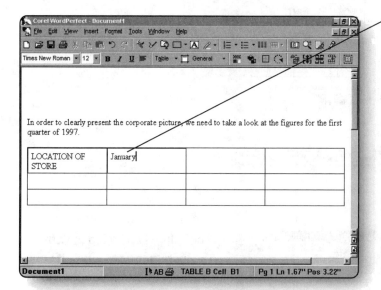

1. **Type** the **beginning value** (Monday, January, Qtr 1, 1st Quarter, etc) in a cell of the table.

NOTE

If you are going to increment regular numbers, you must enter them into two cells. For example, you must enter 1 in the first cell and 2 in the second cell. WordPerfect needs to pick up a pattern from your numbers.

2. **Select** the **cells** that contain the beginning value and the cells to contain the incrementing values.

TIP

To select cells, click at the beginning of the first cell, hold down the Shift key and press the Right Arrow key across (or down) to the ending cell. The cells will be black when they are selected.

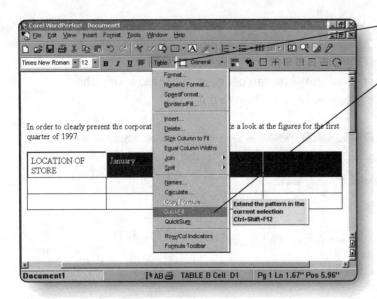

3. **Click** on the **Table button**. The Table menu will appear.

4. **Click** on **QuickFill**.

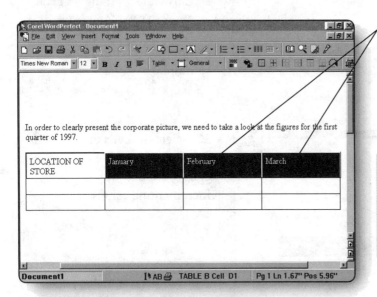

The cells will be filled in with the incrementing values. If you typed an abbreviation for the month or day, WordPerfect will use the corresponding abbreviations.

TIP

To deselect cells in a table, click anywhere in the table outside the selected area.

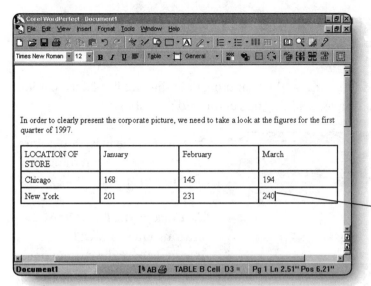

ADDING A ROW AT THE END OF A TABLE

If you need additional rows when you reach the end of your table, WordPerfect can quickly add them for you.

1. Position the **insertion point** at the end of any text in the last cell of the table.

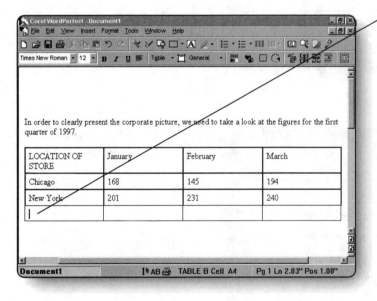

2. Press the **Tab key.** A new row will be added to the end of the table.

3. Repeat steps 1 and **2** for as many additional rows as needed.

ADDING A ROW ELSEWHERE IN A TABLE

Adding a row at the beginning or in the middle of a table is just as simple as adding one at the end of a table.

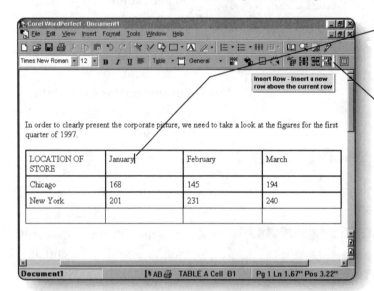

1. **Position** the **insertion point** in any cell where you want the new row to appear.

2. **Click** on the **Insert Row button**. A new row will be inserted above the current one.

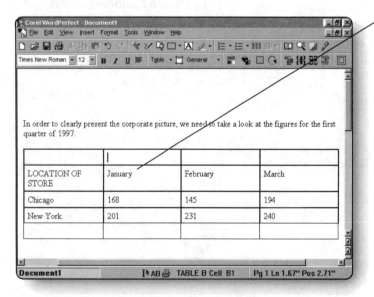

Notice how the existing rows were moved down in the table.

ADDING A COLUMN TO A TABLE

A column can be inserted anywhere in the table.

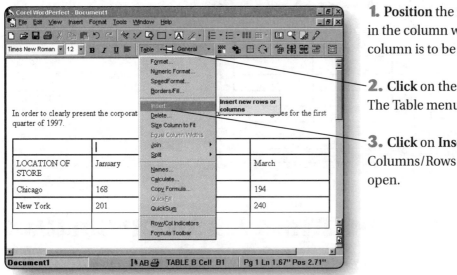

1. Position the **insertion point** in the column where the new column is to be placed.

2. Click on the **Table button**. The Table menu will appear.

3. Click on **Insert**. The Insert Columns/Rows dialog box will open.

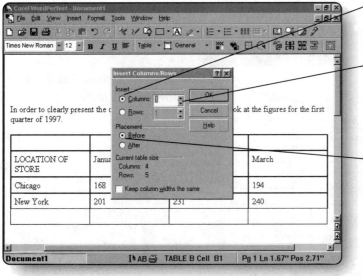

4. Click on **Columns** in the Insert area.

5. Click on the **up and down arrows** (◆) until the box reads the number of columns you want to insert.

6. Click on **Before** in the Placement area.

7. Click on **OK**. The new columns will be inserted into the table.

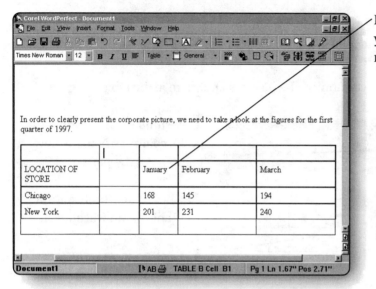

Notice how the column you had your insertion point in has been moved to the right.

DELETING A ROW OR COLUMN

Unwanted rows or columns can be deleted quickly.

1. **Position** the **insertion point** in the row or column you want to delete.

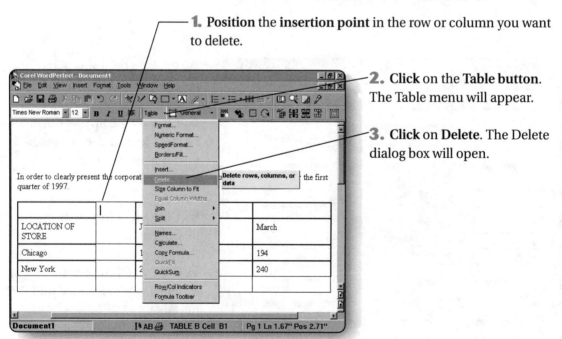

2. **Click** on the **Table button**. The Table menu will appear.

3. **Click** on **Delete**. The Delete dialog box will open.

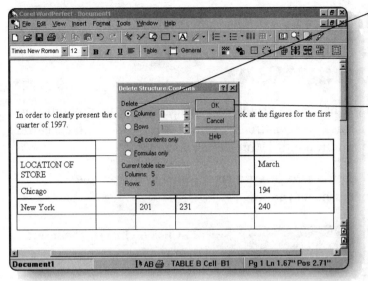

4. Click on **Columns** or **Rows** in the Delete area, depending on whether you want to delete a row or a column.

5. Click on **OK**. The dialog box will close.

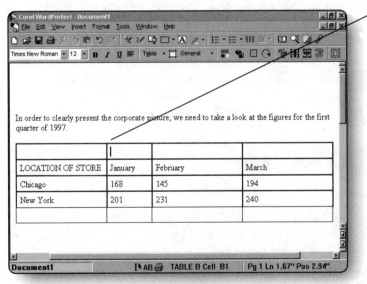

The unwanted row or column will be deleted and existing rows or columns will be pulled up or over.

INSERTING AN EXISTING SPREADSHEET INTO A DOCUMENT

If you have already created a spreadsheet in another program such as Corel Quattro Pro, Lotus 1-2-3, or Microsoft Excel you can insert it into a WordPerfect document.

1. Position the **insertion point** where you want the spreadsheet to appear.

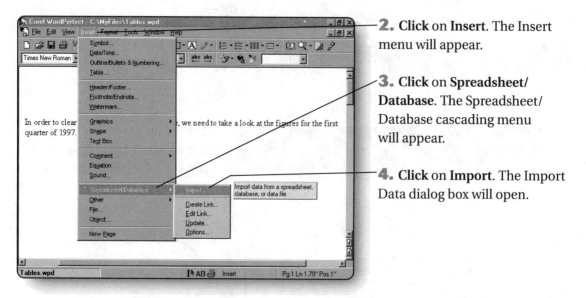

2. **Click** on **Insert**. The Insert menu will appear.

3. **Click** on **Spreadsheet/ Database**. The Spreadsheet/ Database cascading menu will appear.

4. **Click** on **Import**. The Import Data dialog box will open.

NOTE

If you choose Create Link instead of Import, the spreadsheet will be linked to the WordPerfect document. This means that if you update the original spreadsheet, WordPerfect will update the copy in your document the next time you open it. If you Import only, the WordPerfect document does not get updated if the original spreadsheet changes.

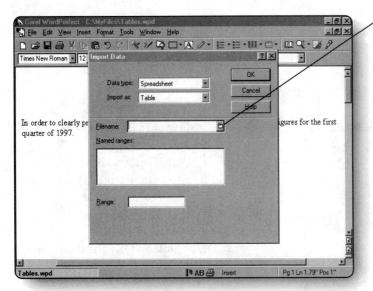

5. Click on the **Browse button** in the Filename: text box. The Select Data Filename dialog box will open.

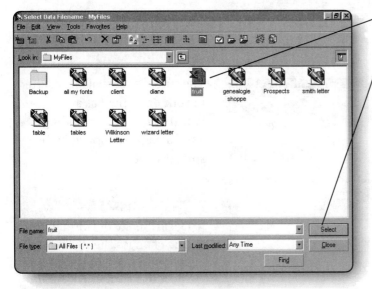

6. Click on the **filename** of your spreadsheet.

7. Click on **Select**. The dialog box will close and the filename will be inserted into the Import Data dialog box.

8. Type the **cell locations** of the spreadsheet you want to import in the Range: text box. Either type a range like B5:C16 or choose a range from the Named Ranges: box.

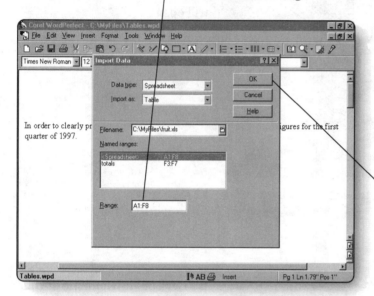

NOTE

If you do not specify a specific range area, WordPerfect will assume you want to import the entire spreadsheet.

9. **Click** on **OK**. The dialog box will close.

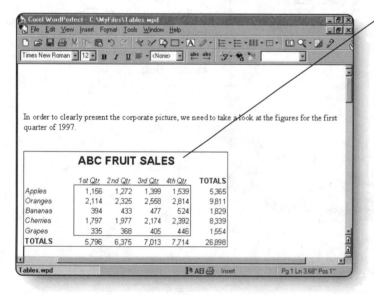

The spreadsheet will be inserted in your document as a WordPerfect table including any formatting applied in the spreadsheet.

NOTE

Occasionally the formatting changes slightly in the conversion from spreadsheet to WordPerfect table. You will still be able to modify it in WordPerfect if that happens.

16 Formatting a Table

The appearance of a WordPerfect table can be changed. You can quickly change the way a table looks by applying a style to the whole table or you can also change the look of specific parts of the table, such as a border or certain cells. In this chapter, you'll learn how to:

✦ Format with SpeedFormat

✦ Select parts of a table

✦ Change column width, number alignment, and lines in a table

✦ Format numbers in a table

✦ Join cells for a table heading

FORMATTING WITH SPEEDFORMAT

WordPerfect's SpeedFormat feature gives you 40 different formats to choose from to save you time.

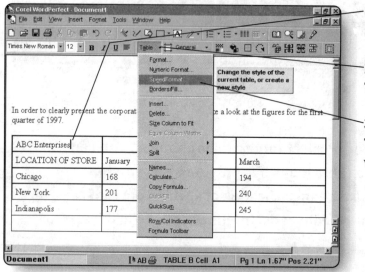

1. Position the **insertion point** anywhere in the table.

2. Click on the **Table button.** The Table menu will appear.

3. Click on **SpeedFormat.** The SpeedFormat dialog box will open.

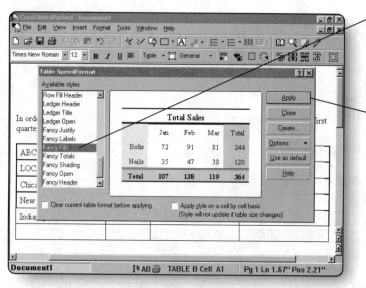

4. Click on **one** of the **Available Styles.** You can see a sample representation in the preview box.

5. Click on **Apply.** The dialog box will close.

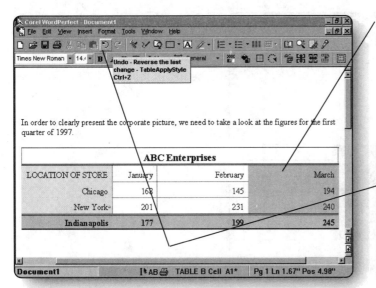

Notice the formatting changes in your table.

SELECTING PARTS OF A TABLE

To modify parts of a table, you need to select the cells you want to change.

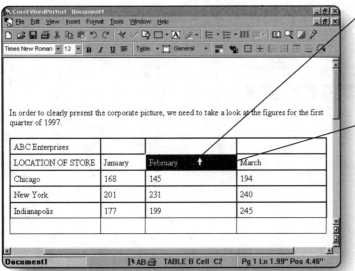

1. **Position** the **mouse pointer** in a cell near the top or left edge. The mouse pointer will turn into a cell selection arrow—a white arrow pointing up or to the left.

2. **Click** on the **mouse button once**. A single cell will be selected.

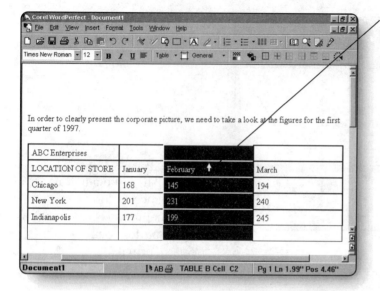

3. With the **cell selection arrow** pointing up, **double-click** the **mouse**. The entire column will be highlighted.

4. With the **cell selection arrow** pointing to the left, **double-click** the **mouse**. The entire row will be highlighted.

NOTE

When a cell or row or column has been selected, you can continue to drag across other cells, rows, or columns to select additional ones.

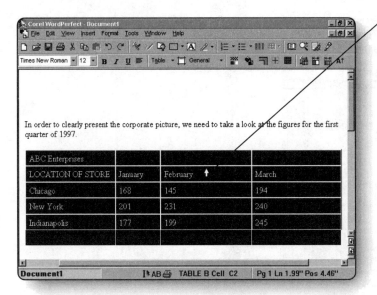

5. With the **cell selection arrow** pointing up or to the left, **triple-click** the **mouse**. The entire table will be highlighted.

CHANGING COLUMN WIDTH IN A TABLE

By default, all columns are equally spaced and a table expands across the entire width of a document. You can change a column to any width you would like, but first you must tell WordPerfect not to expand your table to fill the width of the document.

1. Position the **mouse pointer** anywhere in the table.

2. Click on the **Table button**. The Table menu will appear.

3. Click on **Format**. The Properties for Table Format dialog box will open.

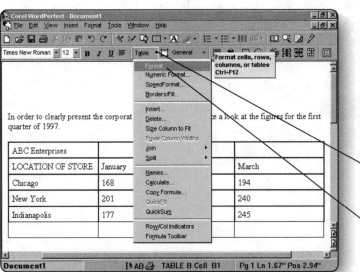

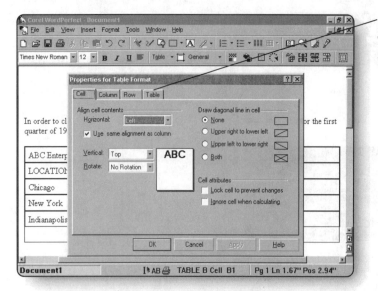

4. Click on the **Table tab**. The Table tab will come to the top of the stack.

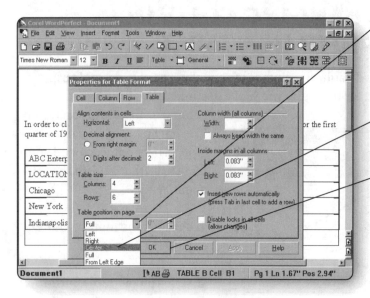

5. Click on the **down arrow** (▼) next to the Table position on page list box. A list of available choices will appear.

6. Click on **Left, Centered,** or **Right**.

7. Click on **OK**. The dialog box will close.

8. **Position** the **mouse pointer** on the line to the right of the column you want to change. The mouse pointer will turn into a black cross with two small arrowheads on it.

9. **Press** and **hold** the **mouse button** and **drag** the **line** to the **left** to make a column smaller or to the **right** to make it wider.

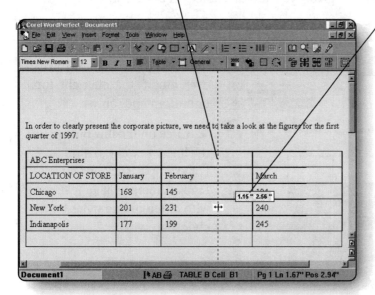

Notice the numbers appearing. These are showing the column widths of both columns on either side of the line you are dragging.

10. **Release** the **mouse button**. The entire column will be changed as well as the column next to it.

11. **Repeat steps** 8 through 10 for all columns you want to change.

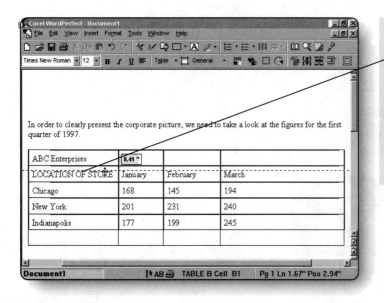

TIP

Row height can be modified the same way by positioning the mouse pointer on the line below the row to be modified and following steps 9 and 10, except drag the line up or down.

CHANGING LINES IN A TABLE

The default choice is to have a single-line border around each cell of a table.

1. **Select** the **cells** you want to modify. The Property Bar will change, giving you several choices of lines to modify.

You can modify the outside lines of your selection, or you can modify the inside lines. You can even modify the left, right, top, or bottom lines only.

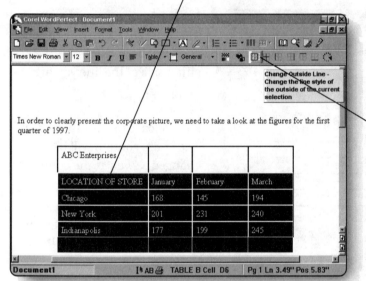

2. **Click** on the **line button** for the line you want to modify. For example, click on Outside Lines. A menu will appear with different line styles to choose from.

3. **Click** on the **style** of **line** best suited for the cells. The selection box will close.

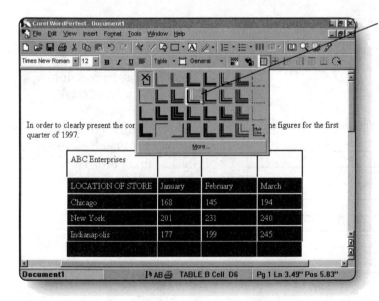

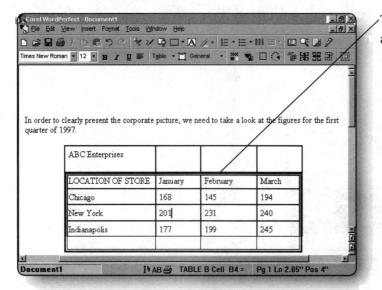

The new line style will be applied to your selection.

FORMATTING NUMBERS IN A TABLE

You have the option of changing the format of any numbers you enter in your table.

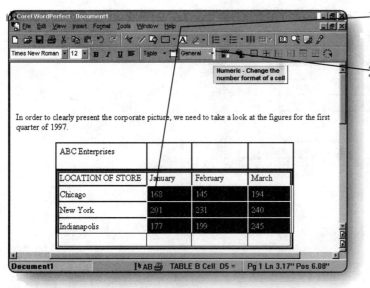

1. **Select** the **cells** you want to modify.

2. **Click** on the **Numeric button**. A list of available formats will appear.

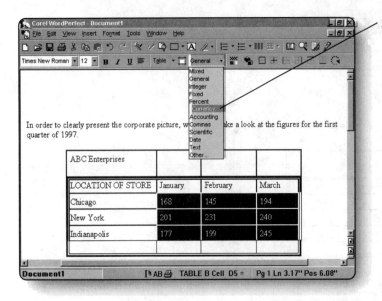

3. Click on a **number style**.

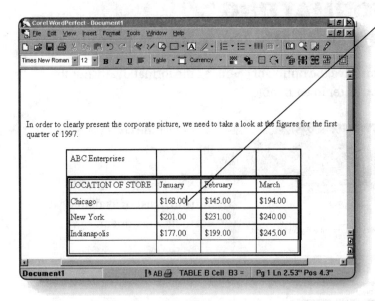

The format you select will be
applied to the highlighted cells.

CHANGING NUMBER ALIGNMENT

Traditionally, numbers are aligned on the right side of a cell.

1. **Select** the **cells** to be modified.

2. **Click** on the **Justification button**. The Justification menu will appear.

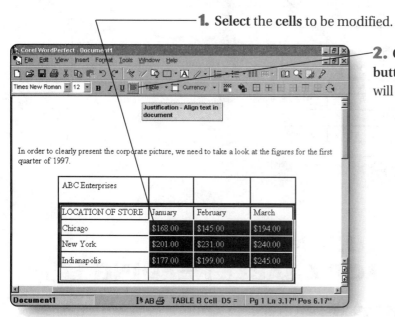

3. **Click** on an **alignment**: Left, Right, Center, Full, or All. The cell alignment will be changed.

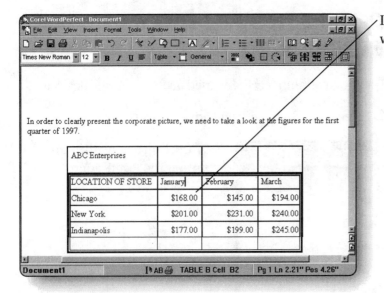

In this figure, the numeric cells were right-aligned.

JOINING CELLS
FOR A TABLE HEADING

Any two or more cells can be joined together to form a larger cell.

1. **Click** on the **QuickJoin button**.

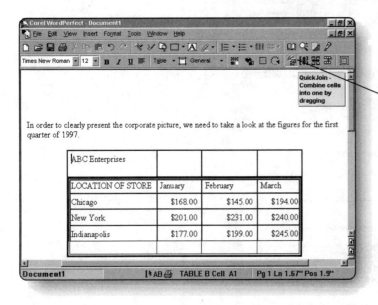

QuickJoin - Combine cells into one by dragging

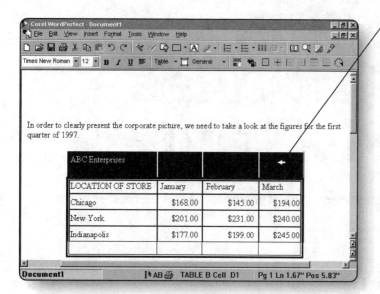

2. Drag the **mouse pointer** across the cells to be joined—for example, the top row of the table.

3. Release the **mouse button**.

The cells will be joined together to form one large cell.

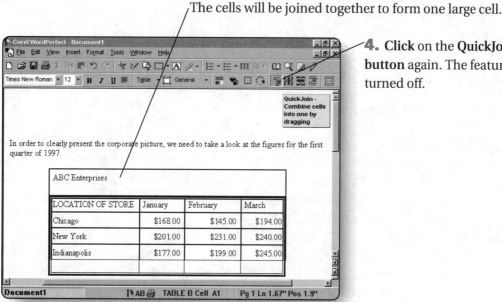

4. Click on the **QuickJoin button** again. The feature will be turned off.

17 Using Formulas in a Table

You can create different kinds of formulas in a WordPerfect table to do your math for you! A formula can do addition, subtraction, multiplication, and division as well as make logical decisions for you. In this chapter, you'll learn how to:

✦ Use QuickSum

✦ Add a column of numbers

✦ Create a simple formula

✦ Copy a formula

USING QUICKSUM

QuickSum is the fastest method to add a sequential column or row of numbers.

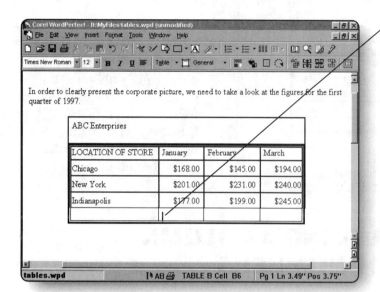

1. Position the **insertion point** in the cell where you want the mathematical answer.

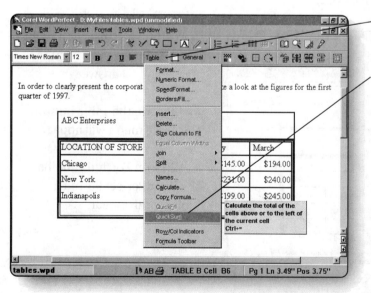

2. Click on the **Table button**. The Table menu will appear.

3. Click on **QuickSum**.

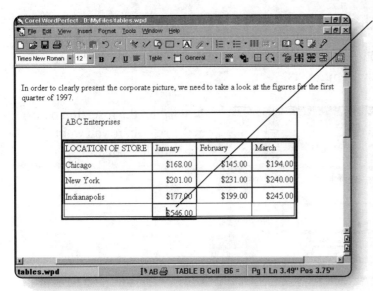

The answer will appear in the empty cell. You may want to modify the alignment and numeric format of the cell.

NOTE

QuickSum will add the numbers directly above the current cell. If there are no numbers directly above it, QuickSum will add the numbers in the cells to the left of the current cell.

ADDING A COLUMN OF NUMBERS

Occasionally, QuickSum cannot determine the cells you want to add up. WordPerfect has a built-in function that will assist you.

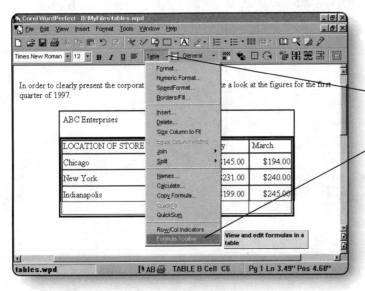

1. **Position** the **insertion point** in the cell where you want the mathematical answer.

2. **Click** on the **Table button**. The Table menu will appear.

3. **Click** on **Formula Toolbar**. The WordPerfect Formula Toolbar will appear.

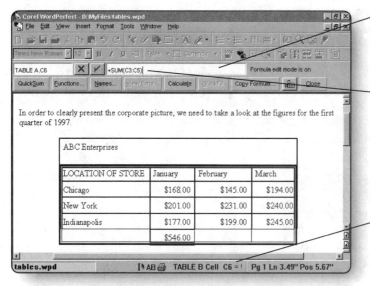

4. Click in the **Formula text box**—the long white box in the Formula Toolbar.

5. Type the following **formula**: **+SUM(xx:XX)**, where xx is the beginning cell address and XX is the ending cell address.

TIP

If you are not sure of a cell's address, look in the Status Bar.

NOTE

WordPerfect tables use addresses just like spreadsheets. The columns are alphabetic—A, B, C, and so on and the rows are numeric—1, 2, 3, and so on. A sample formula for adding part of a column might be +SUM(B2:B16).

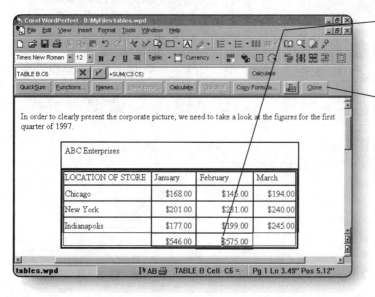

6. Press the **Enter key** to accept the formula. The answer will appear in the current cell.

7. Click on **Close**. The Formula Toolbar will disappear.

Unlike a spreadsheet, WordPerfect does not automatically recalculate a formula if the data changes. You must tell WordPerfect when to recalculate, or to do it all the time.

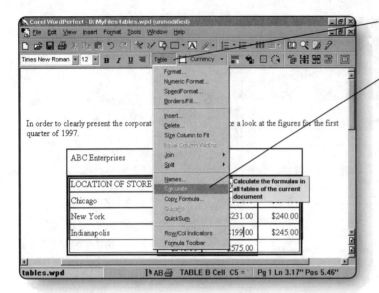

8. **Click** on the **Table button**. The Table menu will appear.

9. **Click** on **Calculate**. The Calculate dialog box will open.

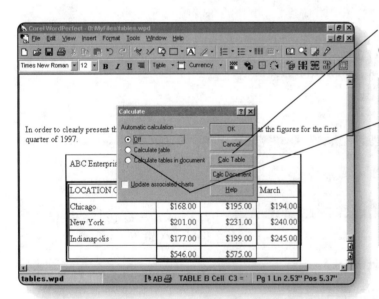

10. **Click** on **Calc Table**. The dialog box will close.

TIP

If you click on Calculate table from the Automatic calculation area, WordPerfect will automatically recalculate any formulas if changes are made to the table.

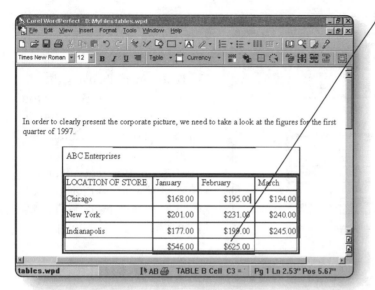

Every formula in the table will be recalculated.

CREATING A SIMPLE FORMULA

Not all formulas involve addition. You can also create formulas to do subtraction, multiplication, or division.

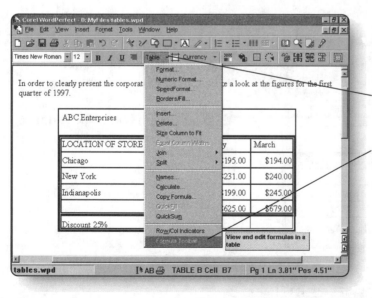

1. **Position** the **insertion point** in the cell where you want the mathematical answer.

2. **Click** on the **Table button.** The Table menu will appear.

3. **Click** on **Formula Toolbar.** The WordPerfect Formula Toolbar will appear.

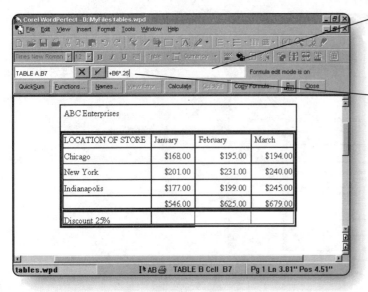

4. **Click** in the **Formula text box**.

5. **Type** a **formula** using the table cells as references. Use the plus sign (+) for addition, the minus sign or hyphen character (-) for subtraction, the asterisk key (*) for multiplication, and the slash key (/) for division. A sample formula might be A3*B5 or C2/C3 or even A3*B3-C3.

NOTE

For a compound formula like the last sample listed in step 5, WordPerfect tables follow the rules of priorities from your old high school algebra class. This means that multiplication and division will be done before addition and subtraction. Put portions of the formula you want calculated first into parentheses to give them priority in a calculation sequence.

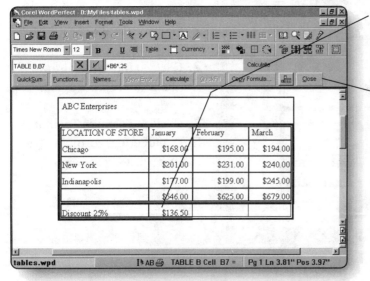

6. **Press** the **Enter key** to accept the formula. The answer will appear in the current cell.

7. **Click** on **Close**. The Formula Toolbar will disappear.

COPYING A FORMULA

It is not necessary to type a formula more than once. Use the Copy Formula feature instead.

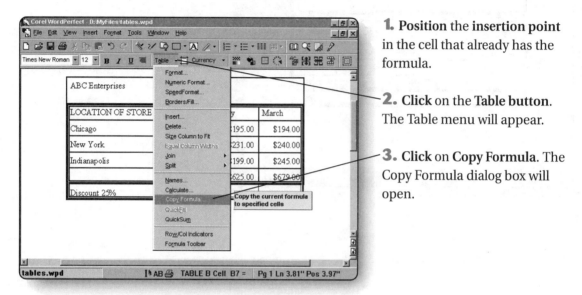

1. Position the **insertion point** in the cell that already has the formula.

2. Click on the **Table button**. The Table menu will appear.

3. Click on **Copy Formula**. The Copy Formula dialog box will open.

4. Click on a **destination**. In our sample figure, we need to copy the formula to the right two times.

From here you can copy the formula to a specific cell.

From here you can copy a formula to the cells below the selected cell.

From here you can copy a formula to the cells to the right of the selected cell.

5. Click on **OK**. The dialog box will close.

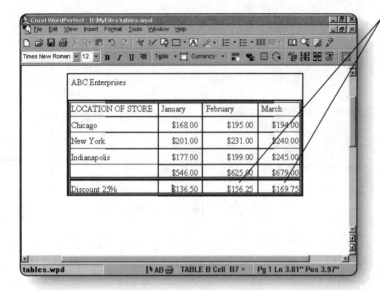

The formula will be duplicated
and the answers inserted in the
desired cells.

18

Creating a Chart from a WordPerfect Table

They say a picture is worth a thousand words, right? A chart can add visual impact to a report, making the information easier to understand. In this chapter, you'll learn how to:

✦ Create a chart

✦ Change the type of chart

✦ Give the chart a title

✦ Change the properties of the legend and chart series

✦ Update chart values

CREATING A CHART

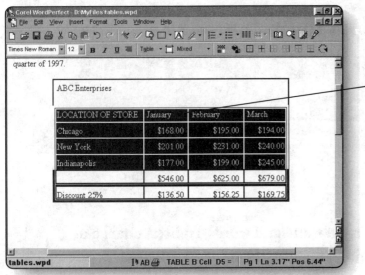

You can plot some or all the data in a WordPerfect table to be included in a chart.

1. **Select** the **cells** to include in the chart.

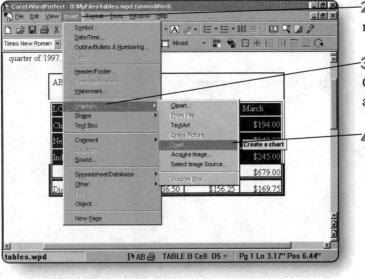

2. **Click** on **Insert**. The Insert menu will appear.

3. **Click** on **Graphics**. The Graphics cascading menu will appear.

4. **Click** on **Chart**.

WordPerfect will launch the Presentations program to create the chart and insert it into your document. Be patient as this may take a couple of minutes depending upon your computer.

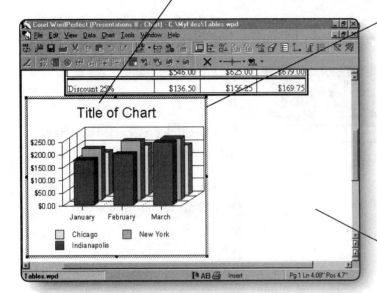

The chart has a small striped frame around it with eight little black boxes in the frame. This means the chart is *active*—that is, you are able to change the attributes of the chart.

The Title Bar also reflects that you are in Presentations and the chart is active.

TIP

If you click anywhere outside the stripped frame of the chart you will deactivate it. To make it active again, double-click anywhere on the chart.

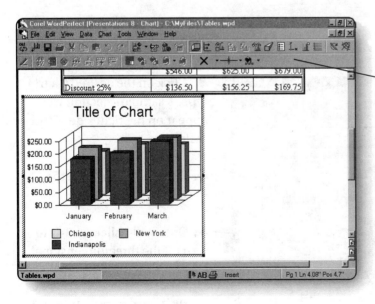

The Toolbar and Property Bar as well as the menu choices have changed to reflect that you are working on a chart.

TIP

To delete a chart you do not want, leave the Presentations portion of the program by clicking anywhere outside the chart boundaries. The chart will have eight small handles around it. Press the Delete key on your keyboard.

CHANGING THE TYPE OF CHART

There are 12 different types of charts available, ranging from pie charts to bar charts to line charts to bubble charts.

The default type of chart is a three-dimensional cluster vertical bar chart.

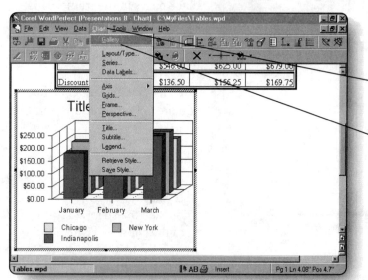

1. **Click** on **Chart**. The Chart menu will appear.

2. **Click** on **Gallery**. The Data Chart Gallery dialog box will open.

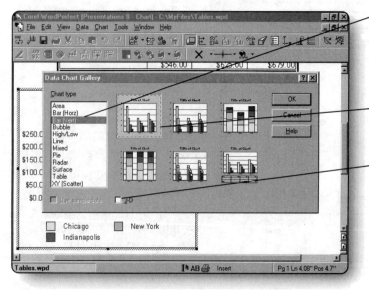

3. **Click** on the desired **Chart type**. A sample selection will appear on the right side of the dialog box.

4. **Click** on a **style** from the samples.

5. Optionally, **click** on **3-D** to turn off the three-dimensional effect.

6. **Click** on **OK**. The chart will change to the selected style.

Bar charts are traditionally used to compare items, while pie charts are used to show parts of a whole unit and line charts usually indicate a trend over a period of time.

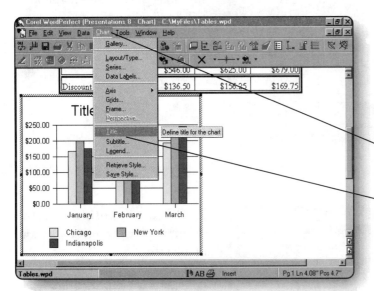

GIVING THE CHART A TITLE

To further identify the topic of the chart, give it a title.

1. **Click** on **Chart**. The Chart menu will appear.

2. **Click** on **Title**. The Title Properties dialog box will open.

3. **Type** the desired **title** in the text box at the top.

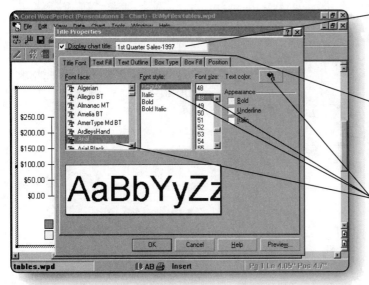

4. **Click** on the desired **font face, style, size,** and **color** for the title.

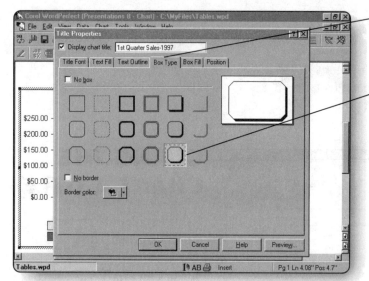

5. **Click** on the **Box Type tab**. The Box Type tab will come to the top of the stack.

6. **Click** on the **type** of **frame** you would like to have around the chart title. A sample frame will be displayed.

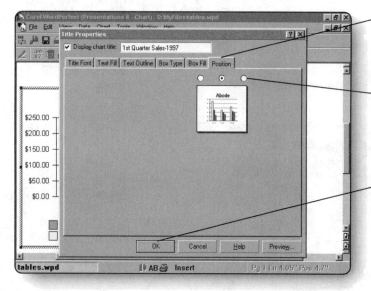

7. **Click** on the **Position tab**. The Position tab will come to the top of the stack.

8. **Click** on a **title position**. You can have the title centered to the chart or over to the left or right side of the chart.

9. **Click** on **OK**. The dialog box will close.

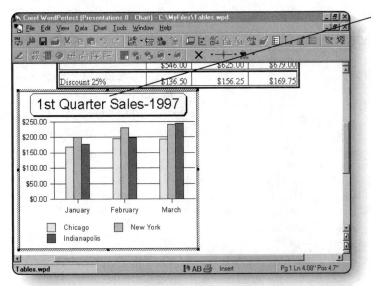

The changes will be made to the chart title.

CHANGING THE PROPERTIES OF THE LEGEND

The legend is an area that identifies the colors and patterns used in the categories of a chart.

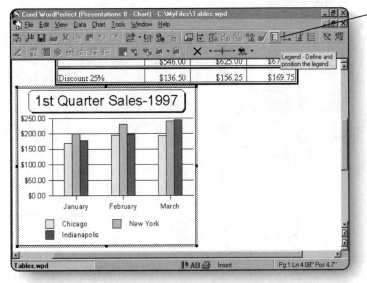

1. Click on the **Legend button**. The Legend dialog box will open.

You have several choices to make about the legend:

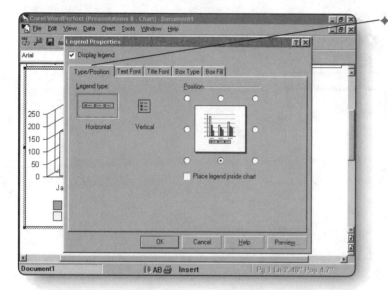

♦ Type/Position will allow you to choose where you want the legend to be in relationship to the chart itself as well as whether the legend is displayed in a vertical or horizontal format.

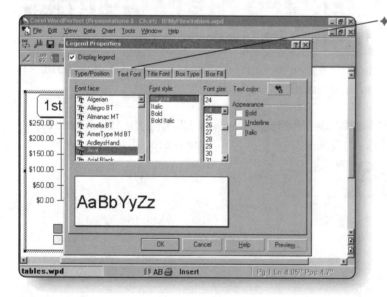

♦ Text Font will allow you to select the font face, style, size, and color for the text in the legend.

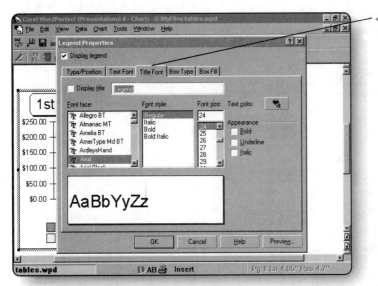

✦ Title Font can give the legend box a title. If you do choose to display a legend title, you can select font properties.

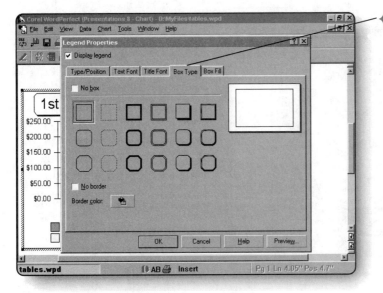

✦ Box Type will allow you to put a box around the legend. There are 18 different styles of boxes to choose from.

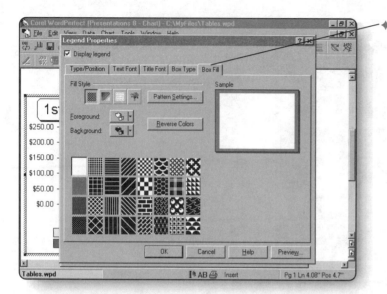

♦ Box Fill will allow you to select a background pattern and color for the box around the legend.

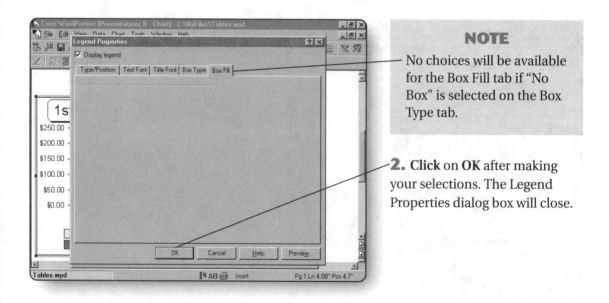

NOTE

No choices will be available for the Box Fill tab if "No Box" is selected on the Box Type tab.

2. **Click** on **OK** after making your selections. The Legend Properties dialog box will close.

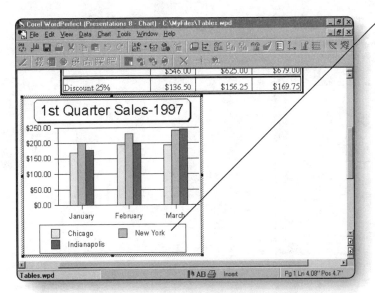

The changes to your legend will go into effect.

CHANGING THE PROPERTIES OF THE CHART SERIES

Suppose you don't like the color or style of the bars in your chart. Change them!

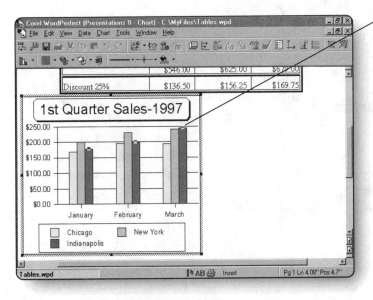

1. **Click** on the **bar series** you want to change. Notice that all bars in that series have a small black box on top of them. The box means that series is selected for changing.

2. **Double-click** on **one** of the **selected bars**. The Series Properties dialog box will open with the Type/Axis tab on top.

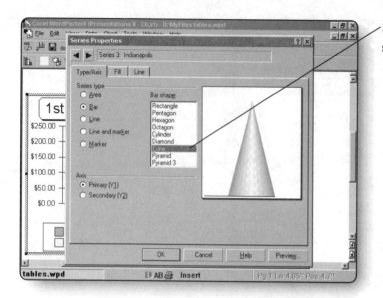

3. Click on a **Bar shape**. A sample will be displayed.

4. Click on the **Fill tab.** It will come back to the top of the stack.

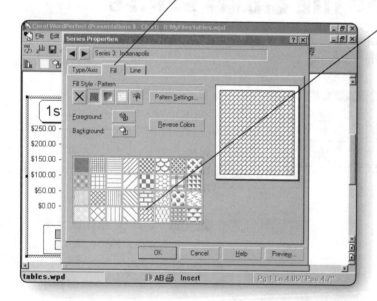

5. Click on a **Fill Style.** This can include patterns, gradient, textures, or pictures.

The choices you see next will vary with your selection in step 5.

TIP

You do not need to choose a background color if the fill pattern is a solid color.

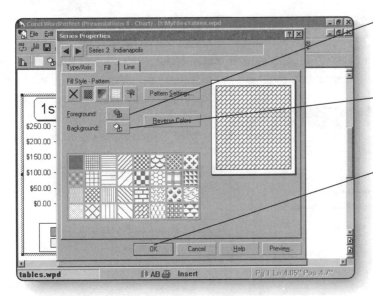

6. Click on a **Foreground color**. This is the primary color in a pattern or gradient.

7. Click on a **Background color**. This is the secondary color in a pattern or gradient.

8. Click on **OK**. The Series Properties dialog box will close.

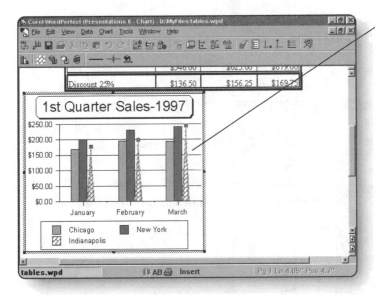

Your chart will be displayed with your changes in it, including the legend.

The chart is considered a graphic element and can be moved or resized. Graphics are covered in Chapter 23.

NOTE

When you have completed making changes to your chart, click anywhere outside of the chart boundaries to deactivate it and return to your WordPerfect document.

UPDATING CHART VALUES

The data in the table are directly tied to the series in the chart. However, if you change a value in the table, the chart will not automatically update. You must tell WordPerfect to go back and recheck the values in the chart.

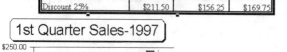
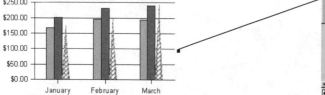

1. Make any **changes** to the WordPerfect table.

2. Click once on the **chart**. It will be selected.

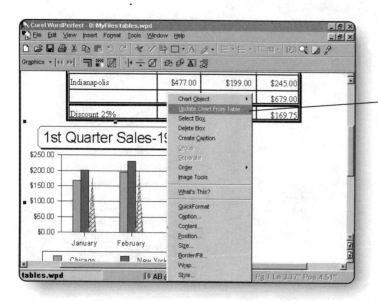

3. Click on the **right mouse button** on top of the chart. A shortcut menu will appear.

4. Click on **Update Chart From Table**. The shortcut menu will close.

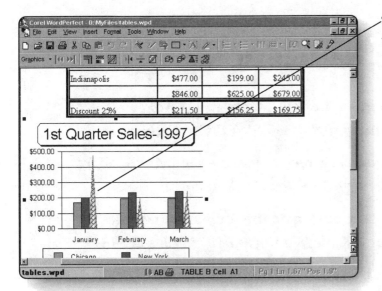

The chart will be updated with the new values.

PART III REVIEW QUESTIONS

1. What is the alignment of the default tabs in a WordPerfect document? *See "Changing the Default Tabs" in Chapter 14*

2. What icon appears on the screen as you are removing a tab from the ruler? *See "Deleting a Tab Stop" in Chapter 14*

3. What is the name of the button on the Toolbar that creates a table? *See "Inserting a Table in a Document" in Chapter 15*

4. What key should be pressed to add a row at the end of a table? *See "Adding a Row at the End of a Table" in Chapter 15*

5. How do you deselect a cell in a table? *See "Selecting Parts of a Table" in Chapter 16*

6. What is the default border in a table? *See "Changing Lines in a Table" in Chapter 16*

7. What is the fastest method to add a sequential column of numbers? *See "Using QuickSum" in Chapter 17*

8. What key is used to designate multiplication in a formula? *See "Creating a Simple Formula" in Chapter 17*

9. What is the default style of chart that WordPerfect will create? *See "Changing the Type of Chart" in Chapter 18*

10. What is a chart legend? *See "Changing the Properties of the Legend" in Chapter 18*

PART IV

Using
Mail Merge

19 Creating an Address List

You know the letter you get from the famous celebrity telling you that you have won TEN MILLION DOLLARS! (OK, in teeny tiny print it says you "may" have won ten million dollars.) It has your name printed in big letters right there on the certificate!

Those letters are created using a feature called Mail Merge. Mail Merge consists of three parts, the first one being a list of names and addresses—called a data file—and the second part being the generic letter called the form file. The last part is the actual merging of part one and part two. We will start with part one of this process. In this chapter, you'll learn how to:

✦ Create a data file

✦ Name data fields

✦ Use Quick Data Entry

✦ Edit a data file

✦ Change a data field name

CREATING A DATA FILE

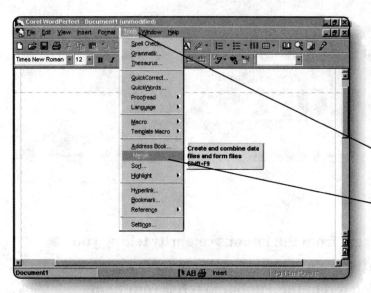

The data file is where your addresses and other variable information will be stored. You need to begin the merge process with a blank document on the screen.

1. Click on **Tools**. The Tools menu will appear.

2. Click on **Merge**. The Merge dialog box will open.

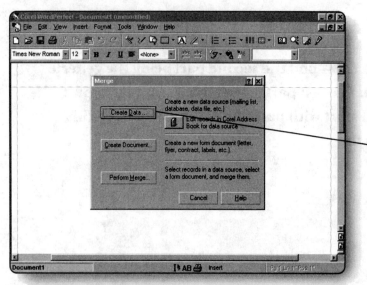

From this dialog box you can create either of the two parts to a mail merge or even complete the process by combining the two together to create the finished letter.

3. Click on **Create Data**. The Create Data File dialog box will open.

NAMING DATA FIELDS

Fields and records are two of the common terms used with merge data files. A *field* is an individual piece of information about someone, such as zip code or first name. A *record* is the complete picture of information about someone with all the fields put together.

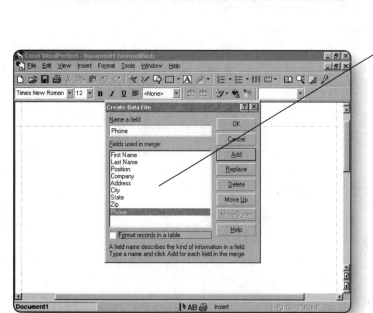

1. Type a **descriptive name** for a field. This is not the actual information such as John, Smith, or 555-1212; it's a title for the pieces of information such as First Name, Last Name, or Phone Number.

2. **Click** on **Add**. The field name will be added to the Fields used in merge: box and you are ready to add another field.

3. **Repeat steps 1** and **2** for as many fields you need for your address list.

You can create the data in a table format. In a table format, each column of the table will contain a field. Each row will contain a record.

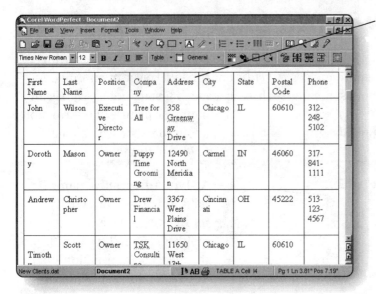

This figure shows what data in a table format will look like.

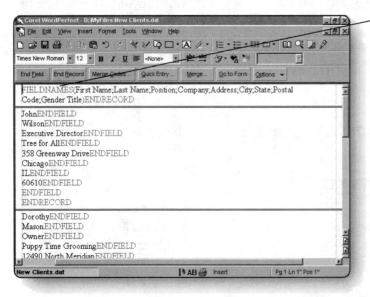

This figure shows what data in a text (nontable) format will look like. This is similar to earlier versions of WordPerfect.

4. Click on **Format records in a table** to turn this feature on. A ✔ will appear in the check box.

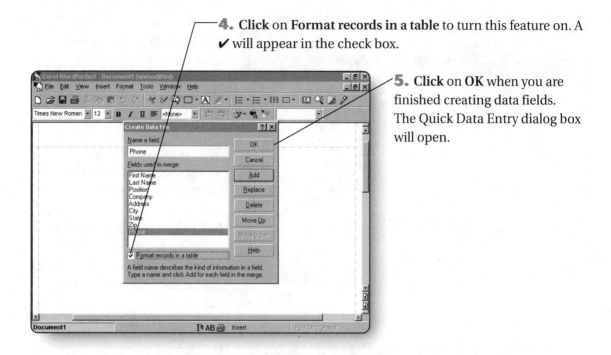

5. Click on **OK** when you are finished creating data fields. The Quick Data Entry dialog box will open.

USING QUICK DATA ENTRY

The Quick Data Entry dialog box is where you will enter the actual information about someone such as name or address.

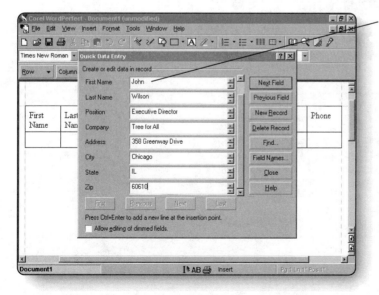

1. Type the **information** for the first field.

2. Press the **Enter key**. The insertion point will move to the next field.

3. Continue typing the information for the first record in the appropriate field, pressing the Enter key to move to the next field.

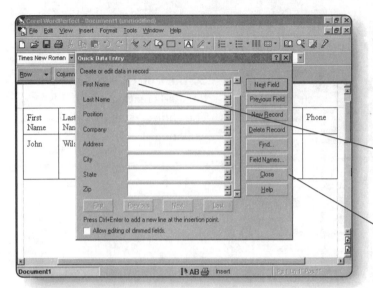

When you have entered the last field of information for this record, WordPerfect automatically gives you another blank record to begin entering the next person's information.

4. **Continue entering** the **records** for your address file following steps 1 through 3.

5. **Click** on the **Close button** when you finish. WordPerfect will prompt you to save your file.

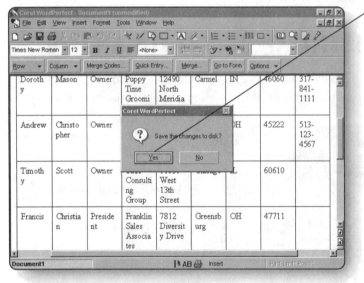

6. **Click** on **Yes** to save this file. The Save File dialog box will open.

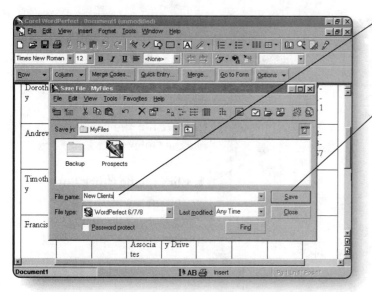

7. Type a **name** for the data file. WordPerfect will add .dat at the end to identify this file as a data file.

8. Click on **Save**. The file will be saved and the dialog box will close.

The filename appears at the top of your screen.

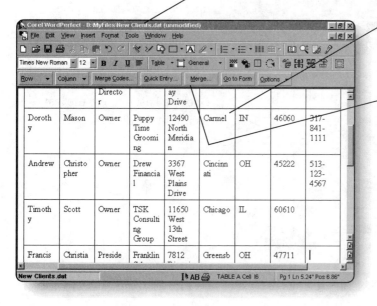

The data is displayed on your screen in the format you selected earlier.

A Merge Tools feature bar appears with buttons specifically for merging.

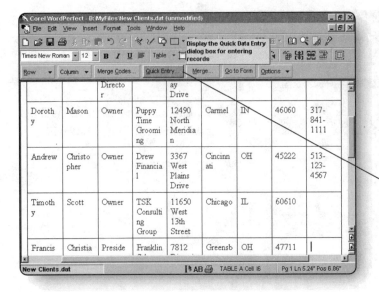

EDITING A DATA FILE

If you need to add or delete a record or change an address in the data file, the fastest way is to use the Quick Data Entry box.

1. **Click** on the **Quick Entry button** on the feature bar. The Quick Data Entry dialog box will appear.

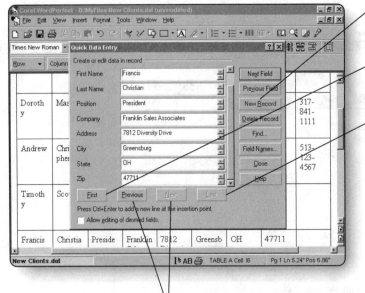

Click on New Record to add a new person to the data file.

Click on First to go to the first record in the data file.

Click on Last to go to the last record in the data file.

Click on Previous or Next to move forward or backward one record in the data file.

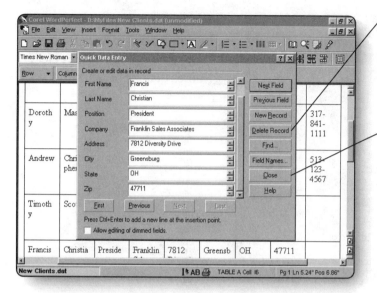

Click on Delete Record to delete the current record.

2. Click in any **field** and **type** any necessary **changes**.

3. Click on **Close**. The Quick Data Entry dialog box will close.

4. Click on **Yes** to save the changes to the data file.

CHANGING FIELD NAMES

You can change, delete, or even add a new field to the data file. You changes will affect all existing records as well as new ones.

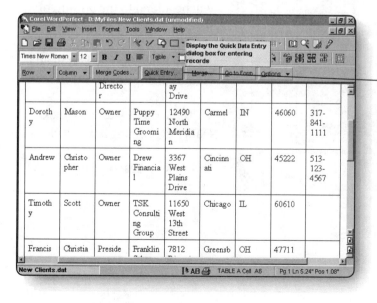

Adding a New Field

1. Click on the **Quick Entry button** on the feature bar. The Quick Data Entry dialog box will appear.

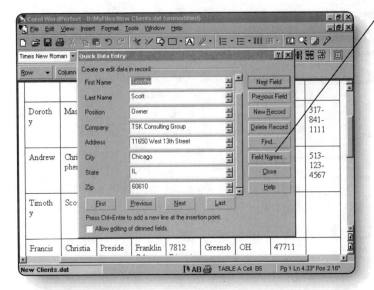

2. Click on the **Field Names button** from the Quick Data Entry dialog box. The Edit Field Names dialog box will open.

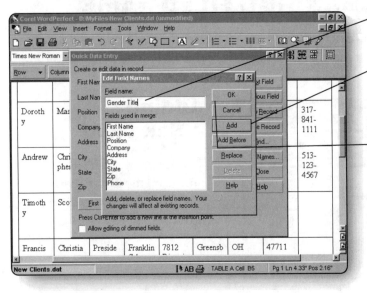

3. Click in the **Field Name: text box** and **type** a new **field name**.

4. Click on **Add**. The field name will be added to the bottom of the list.

5. Click on **OK**. The Edit Field Names dialog box will close.

6. Click on **Close**. The Quick Data Entry dialog box will close.

7. Click on **Yes** to save your changes.

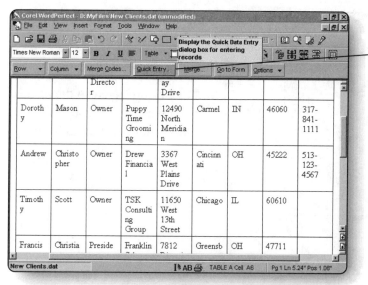

Deleting a Field

1. **Click** on the **Quick Entry button** on the feature bar. The Quick Data Entry dialog box will appear.

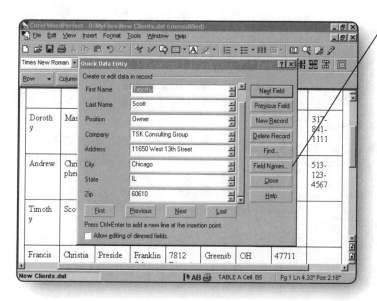

2. **Click** on the **Field Names button** from the Quick Data Entry dialog box. The Edit Field Names dialog box will open.

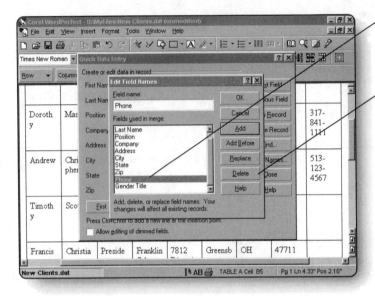

3. **Click** on the **field name** to delete from the Fields used in merge: scroll box.

4. **Click** on **Delete**. A dialog box will open warning you that the field contents will be deleted from every existing record.

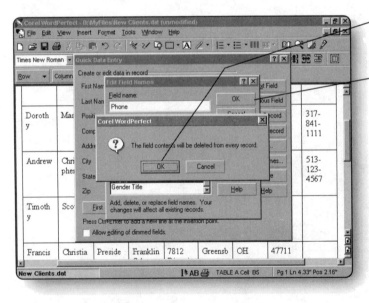

5. **Click** on **OK**. That field will be deleted.

6. **Click** on **OK**. The Edit Field Names dialog box will close.

7. **Click** on **Close**. The Quick Data Entry dialog box will close.

8. **Click** on **Yes** to save your changes.

Renaming a Field

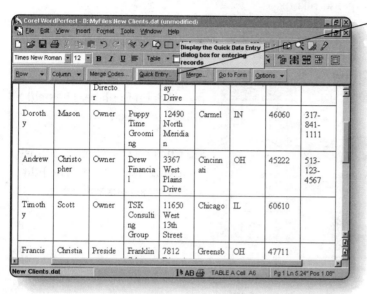

1. Click on the **Quick Entry button** on the feature bar. The Quick Data Entry dialog box will appear.

2. Click on the **Field Names button** from the Quick Data Entry dialog box. The Edit Field Names dialog box will open.

3. Click on the **field name** to rename from the Fields used in merge: scroll box.

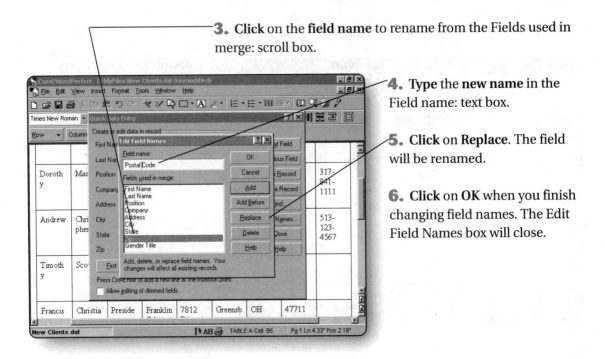

4. Type the **new name** in the Field name: text box.

5. Click on **Replace**. The field will be renamed.

6. Click on **OK** when you finish changing field names. The Edit Field Names box will close.

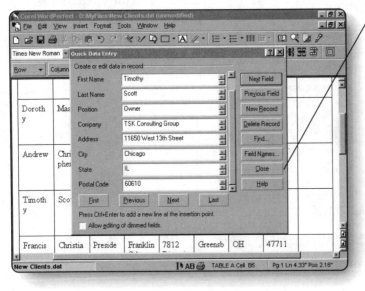

7. Click on **Close**. The Quick Data Entry dialog box will close.

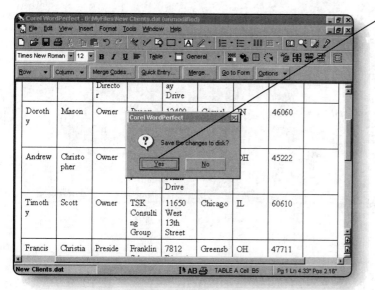

8. Click on **Yes** to save your changes. Your data file will be modified according to your selections.

20 Creating a Form Letter

The second step in Mail Merge is creating the form letter. The form document contains the information that will not change from letter to letter. It will also include *data fields* to tell WordPerfect where to put the information from the data file. In this chapter, you'll learn how to:

✦ Create a form letter

✦ Use automatic dates

✦ Insert data fields

CREATING A FORM LETTER

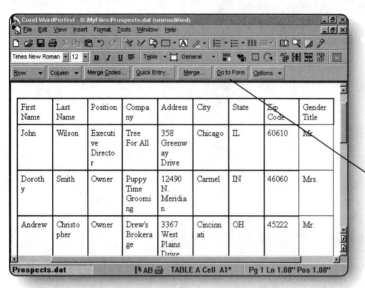

First you need to *associate* the data file with a form file. When you merge that form file in the future, the associated source file is used.

1. **Open** the **data file** you have already created.

2. **Click** on the **Go To Form button** on the Merge feature bar. A dialog box will open advising you that WordPerfect doesn't know which form file to associate with the open data file.

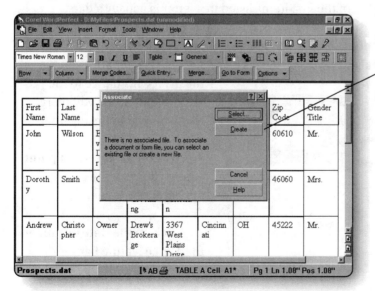

You can either select an existing file or create a new one.

3. **Click** on **Create** to create a new file.

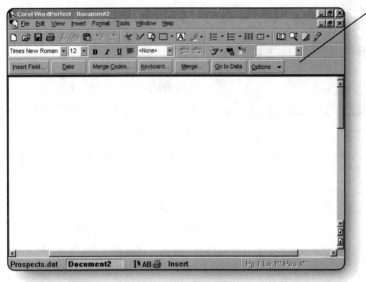

A blank WordPerfect document will open on the screen, with the Merge feature bar displayed.

USING AUTOMATIC DATES

One of the first items listed in a letter is usually a date. WordPerfect gives you two types of dates to use. You learned about using a *date text* in Chapter 1. Another type of date is called the *merge date*. The merge date is *dynamic*, which means it will change to the current date when you merge the two documents together.

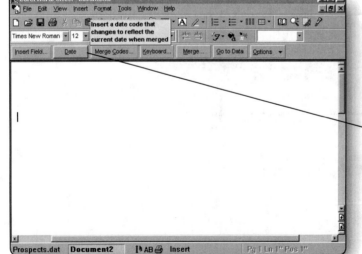

1. **Position** the **insertion point** where you want the date to appear in the letter.

2. **Click** on the **Date button** on the Merge feature bar.

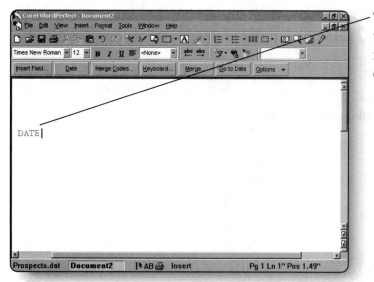

The word "DATE" will appear in the document in red letters. In reality, this is a WordPerfect code.

INSERTING DATA FIELDS

You are now ready to tell WordPerfect where to insert the data from the data file you created. Because of the association you made earlier in this chapter, WordPerfect knows what field names you used in your data file.

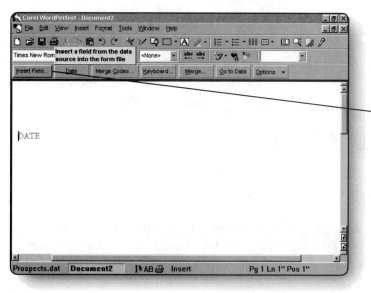

1. **Position** the **insertion point** where you want the first field of information to appear in the letter.

2. **Click** on the **Insert Field button** on the Merge feature bar. The Insert Field Name or Number dialog box will open.

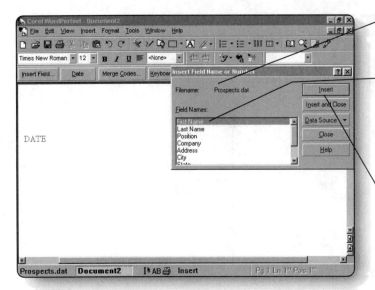

The data file associated with this letter.

The field names from the associated data file.

3. **Click** on the first **data field** you want in your letter.

4. **Click** on **Insert**. The field name will be inserted into your document and the dialog box will remain open.

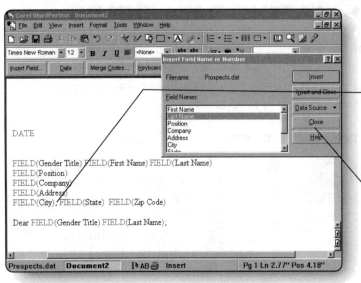

5. **Repeat steps 1, 3,** and 4 for each additional field in your letter.

You will need to add punctuation as necessary between the fields, but not in the actual fields.

6. **Click** on the **Close button**. The Insert Field Name or Number dialog box will close.

NOTE

You do not have to use every field in the form file, and you can use fields more than once. In this example, I used the Gender Title and Last Name fields twice.

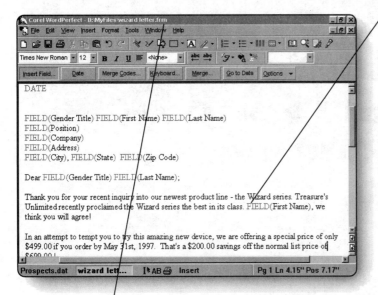

7. Continue typing the body of your letter as desired. Data fields can be inserted in the body of the letter as well as at the beginning.

8. Save the **form letter**. WordPerfect will assign .frm to the end of the filename to designate it as a form letter.

21 Putting an Address List and Form Letter Together

It's time to put the first two elements of a Mail Merge together—the data source and the form letter. In this chapter, you'll learn how to:

✦ Merge names and addresses with a letter

✦ Merge to specific conditions

✦ Merge to selected records

✦ Create envelopes for the merged records

MERGING NAMES AND ADDRESSES WITH A LETTER

Merging is the final step to this process. The merge process will create a separate letter for each record in the data file.

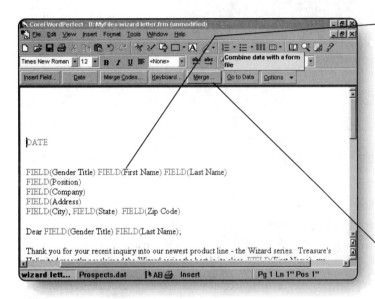

1. **Open** the **form file**. To follow along with this example, use the form letter you created in the previous chapter.

> ### NOTE
>
> The data file does not have to be open, but the merge will still work just fine if it is open.

2. **Click** on the **Merge button** on the Merge feature bar. The Perform Merge dialog box will open.

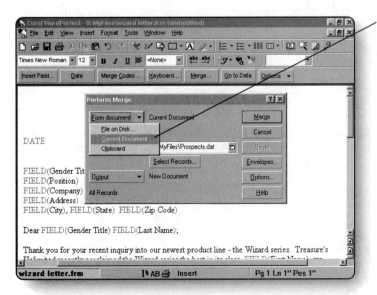

The Form Document button allows you to select which form letter you are using.

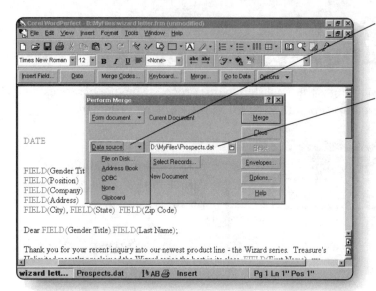

The Data Source button allows you to select the location of the data file

Notice the link to your sample data file.

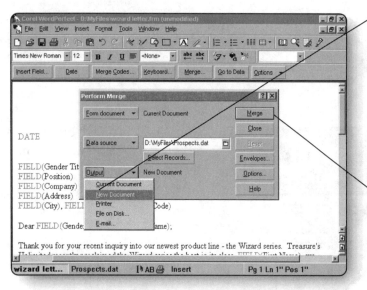

The Output Button allows you to direct the final merge.

> **TIP**
> I recommend merging to a new document first to double-check for any errors.

3. **Click** on the **Merge button** to perform the merge process.

4. **Press** the **Ctrl + Home keys** to go to the beginning of the merged document.

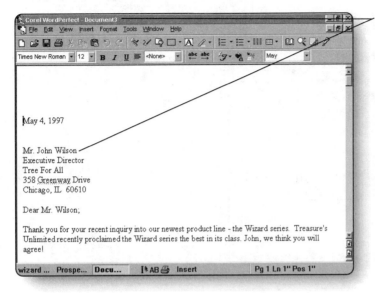

A new document has been created with one letter for each record in the data file.

You will now want to examine the document for any errors or omissions you may have made in the form or data file. If you find any problems, close the merged file, correct the errors, and merge again.

MERGING TO SPECIFIC CONDITIONS

WordPerfect allows you to choose which records you want to merge with the form letter. Perhaps you only want to send this letter to the people who live in a certain city, say Chicago, or only the people who have a last name of Smith.

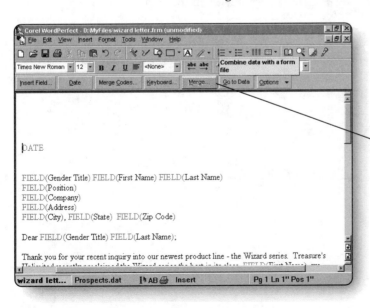

1. **Open** the **form letter**.

2. **Click** on the **Merge button** on the Merge feature bar. The Perform Merge dialog box will open.

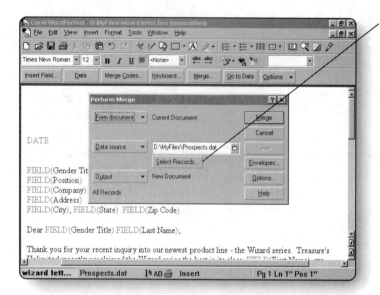

3. **Click** on the **Select Records button.** The Select Records dialog box will open.

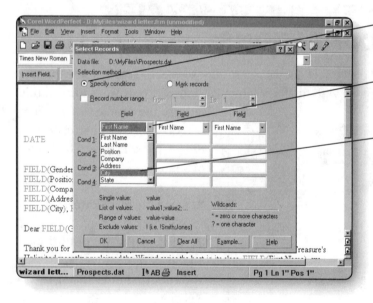

4. **Click** on **Specify Conditions** (if it is not already selected).

5. **Click** on the **down arrow (▼)** in the first field column.

6. **Click** on the **field** from which you want to specify the records.

7. Type the **condition** in the Cond 1: text box. For example, if you want only the records of people who live in Chicago, then just type Chicago in the Cond 1: text box.

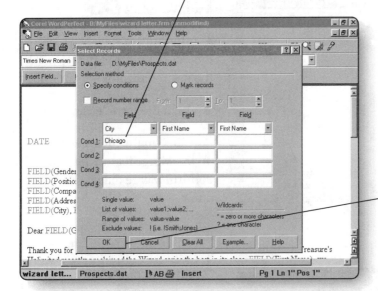

8. Click on **OK**. The Select Records dialog box will close and you will return to the Perform Merge dialog box.

9. Click on **Merge**. The merge will be performed according to the criteria you specified.

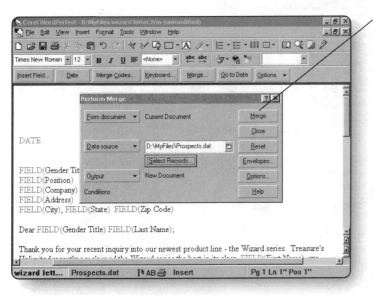

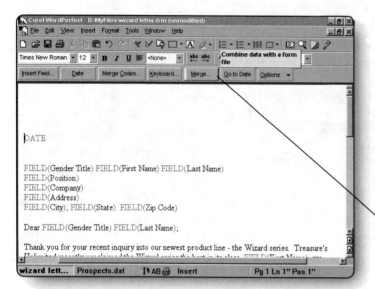

MERGING TO SELECTED RECORDS

Another way to specify which records to merge with is to mark the desired records.

1. **Open** the **form letter**.

2. **Click** on the **Merge button** on the Merge feature bar. The Perform Merge dialog box will open.

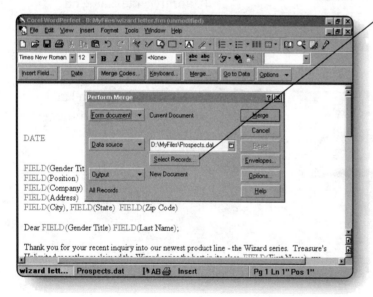

3. **Click** on the **Select Records button**. The Select Records dialog box will open.

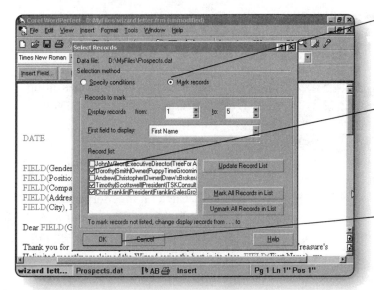

4. Click on **Mark Records**. The dialog box will change to show a representation of each record in the data file.

5. Click on the **names** of the records you want to merge from the Record list: box. A ✔ will appear beside each name you choose.

6. Click on **OK**. The Select Records dialog box will close and you will return to the Perform Merge dialog box.

7. Click on **Merge**. The merge will be performed with the records you selected.

CREATING ENVELOPES FOR THE MERGED RECORDS

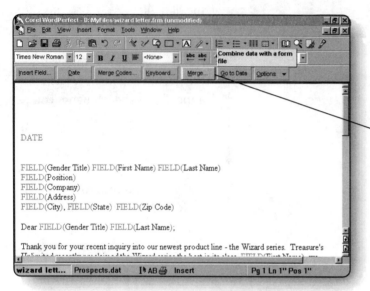

You can create envelopes along with the letter each time you merge.

1. **Open** the **form letter**.

2. **Click** on the **Merge button** on the Merge feature bar. The Perform Merge dialog box will open.

3. **Click** on the **Envelopes button**. The Envelopes dialog box will open with a sample envelope displayed.

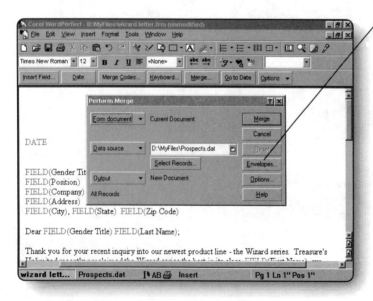

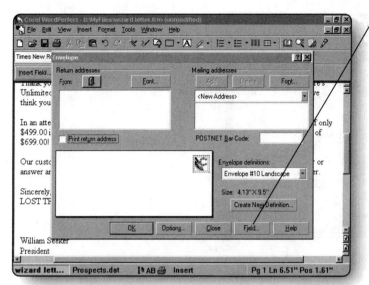

4. Click on the **Field button**. A dialog box of available fields will open.

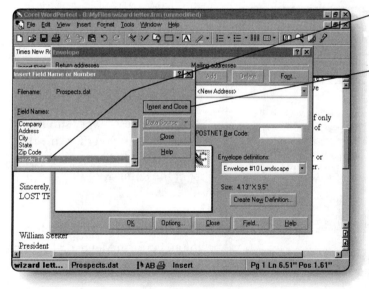

5. Click on the **first field name** to be inserted in the envelope.

6. Click on **Insert and Close**. The dialog box will close.

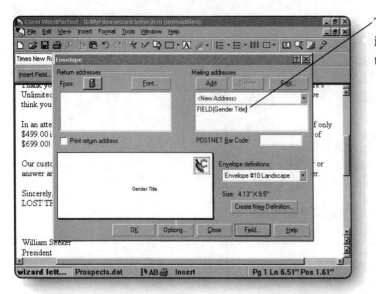

The field name will be inserted in the Mailing addresses area of the envelope.

7. Repeat steps **4** through **6** as needed to insert the proper fields in the envelope.

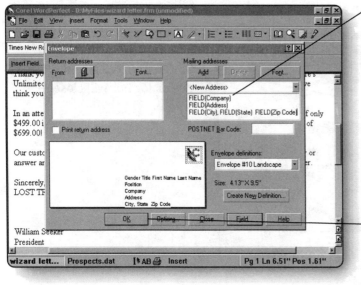

8. Click on **OK**. You will return to the Perform Merge dialog box.

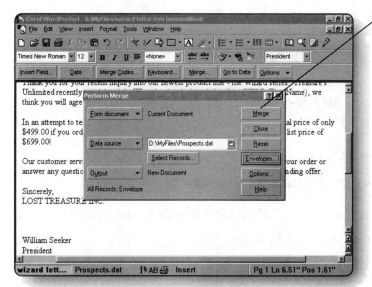

9. **Click** on the **Merge button.** WordPerfect will perform the actual merge.

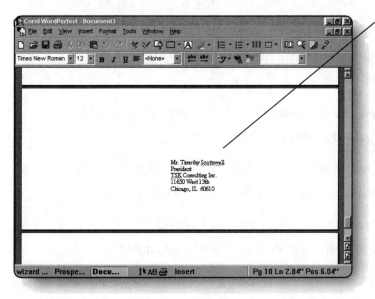

All the letters will be listed together, followed by all the envelopes at the bottom of the new document.

PART IV REVIEW QUESTIONS

1. **What is stored in a data file?** *See "Creating a Data File" in Chapter 19*

2. **If you create your data file as a table, what is stored in each column?** *See "Naming Data Fields" in Chapter 19*

3. **What letters are added to the end of a data file when you save it?** *See "Using Quick Data Entry" in Chapter 19*

4. **What type of information is stored in the form document?** *See "Creating a Form Letter" in Chapter 20*

5. **What does an "association" do?** *See "Creating a Form Letter" in Chapter 20*

6. **What does a dynamic merge date do?** *See "Using Automatic Dates" in Chapter 20*

7. **Does every field in a data file need to be inserted into the form file?** *See "Inserting Data Fields" in Chapter 20*

8. **Does the data file need to be opened before you can merge?** *See "Merging Names and Addresses with a Letter" in Chapter 21*

9. **Why should you merge to a new document before you print?** *See "Merging Names and Addresses with a Letter" in Chapter 21*

10. **Which item will print first during a merge—letters or envelopes?** *See "Creating Envelopes for the Merged Records" in Chapter 21*

PART V

Getting Creative with Graphics

22 Working with Graphic Lines

WordPerfect has a new drawing layer feature that includes the ability to add horizontal, vertical, or diagonal lines of any size, thickness, or color anywhere in your document. You can also add shaped objects such as arrows, rectangles, polygons, or circles. In this chapter, you'll learn how to:

✦ Add and move a graphic line

✦ Edit the thickness, style, and attributes of a graphic line

✦ Delete a graphic line

✦ Add an arrow

ADDING A GRAPHIC LINE

You can add a horizontal or vertical line. Once you know how to do that, it's easy to work with diagonal lines and other shapes.

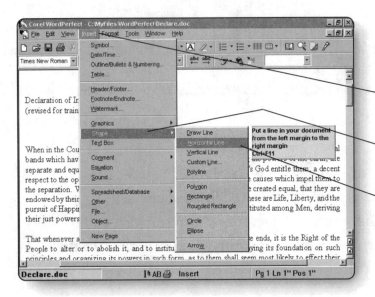

1. **Position** the **insertion point** in the document where you want the graphic line to appear.

2. **Click** on **Insert**. The Insert menu will appear.

3. **Click** on **Shape**. The Shape cascading menu will appear.

4. **Click** on **Horizontal Line** or **Vertical Line**. A line will be inserted into your document at the position of the insertion point.

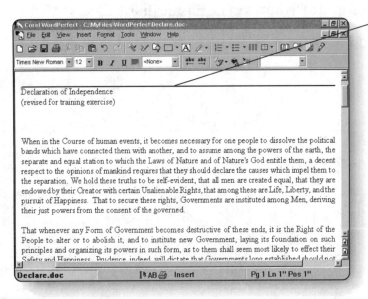

If you selected Horizontal Line, a line will be inserted in your document from the left margin to the right margin.

OR

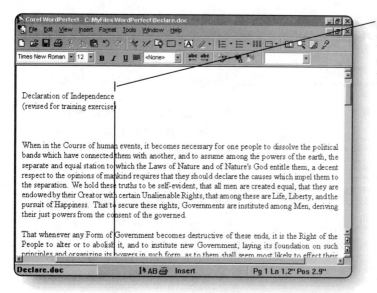

If you selected Vertical Line, a line will be inserted in your document from the top to the bottom margin.

MOVING A GRAPHIC LINE

If you inserted the graphic line at the wrong position in your document, you can move it.

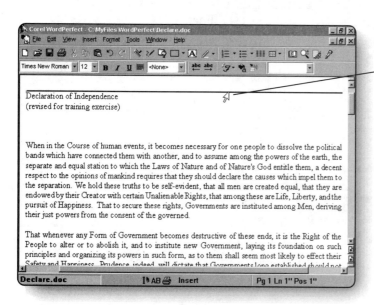

TIP

To select the graphic line, make sure the mouse pointer is in the shape of a white arrow, not the standard I-beam you normally see when working in a document.

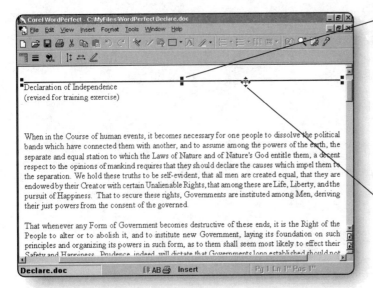

1. **Click** on the **graphic line**. The graphic line will be selected and you will see six black boxes called *handles* around the line.

Notice the change in the Property Bar. It now reflects choices applicable to graphic lines.

2. **Position** the **mouse pointer** anywhere on the line but not on the little black boxes. The mouse pointer will turn into a cross with four arrowheads on it.

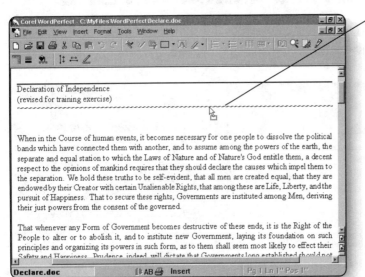

3. **Click** and **drag** the line to the new position. A dotted line will show the new position of the line.

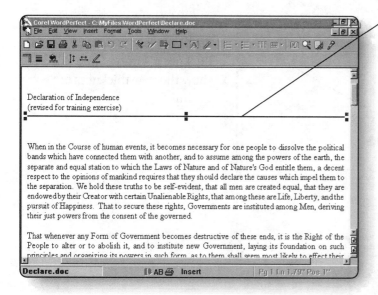

4. **Release** the **mouse button**. The line will be dropped into the new position.

CHANGING THE THICKNESS OF A GRAPHIC LINE

By default, a graphic line is .013" thick, or *hairline* thickness. You can change the thickness of the line to whatever you would like.

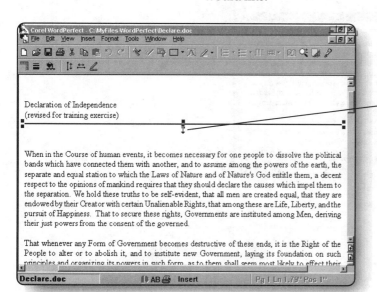

1. **Click** on the **graphic line**. Six black handles will appear around the line.

2. **Position** the **mouse pointer** on any of the handles. The mouse pointer will turn into a double-headed arrow.

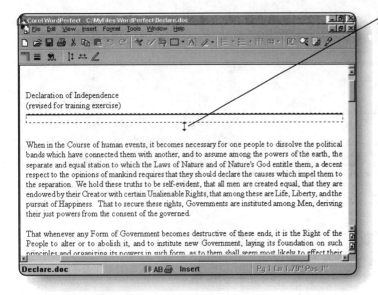

3. **Click** and **drag** the handle until you get the desired thickness. A dotted line will show the new thickness of the line.

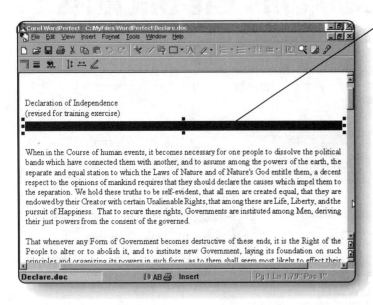

4. **Release** the **mouse button**. The dotted line will disappear and the line will be changed to the new thickness.

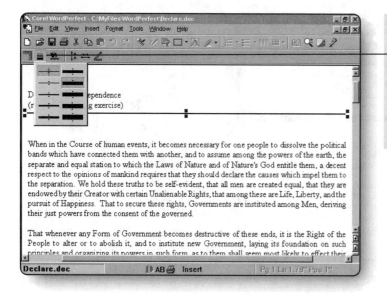

CHANGING THE STYLE OF A GRAPHIC LINE

A graphic line is a single line by default, but there are 32 different styles you can apply.

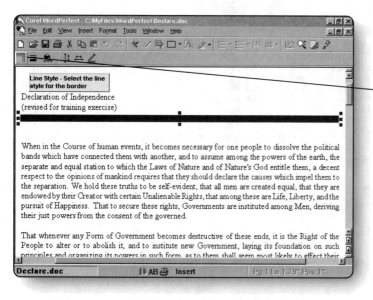

1. **Click** on the **graphic line**. Six black handles will appear around the line.

2. **Click** on the **Line Style button**. A box will appear with many of the line style choices.

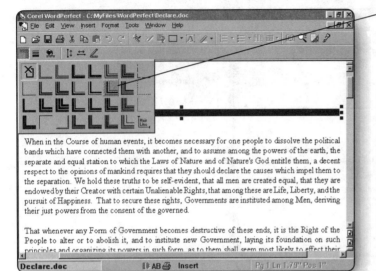

3. Click on the **style** of **line** you would like for your graphic line. The selection box will close.

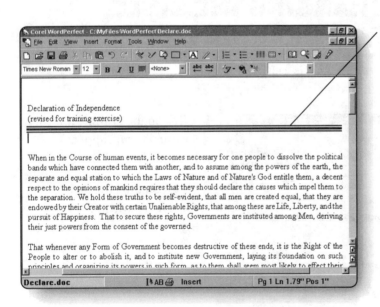

The line will change to the style you selected.

EDITING THE ATTRIBUTES OF A GRAPHIC LINE

You can change all the attributes of a line from one dialog box, including the color, thickness, and style.

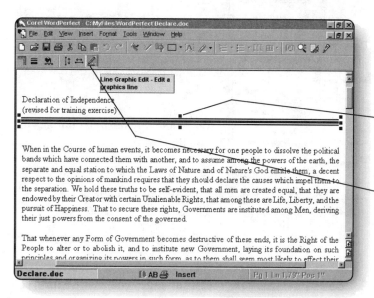

1. Click on the **graphic line**. Six black handles will appear around the line.

2. Click on the **Line Graphic Edit button**. The Edit Graphics Line dialog box will open.

There are many changes you can make from this dialog box.

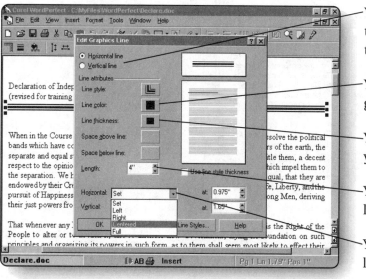

You can change a horizontal line to a vertical line or a vertical line to a horizontal line.

You can change the color of your graphic line.

You can change the thickness of your graphic line.

You can change the length of the line.

You can set the position of your line on the page.

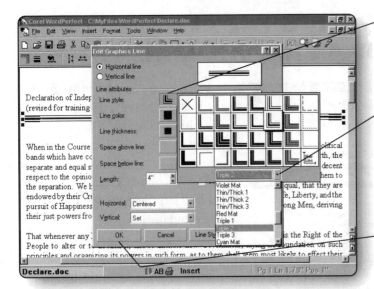

You can change the style of your graphic line.

3. **Make** any desired **changes** to the line.

4. **Click** on **OK**. The Edit Graphic Line dialog box will close.

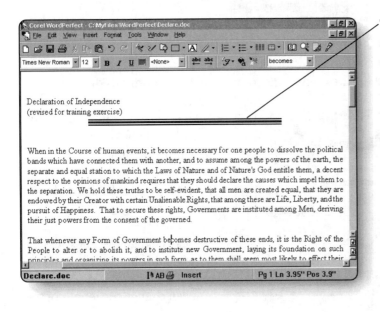

The changes you made will appear. In this example, I changed the length to four inches and centered the line.

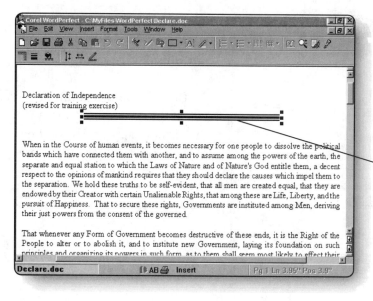

DELETING A GRAPHIC LINE

If you no longer want the graphic line in your document, you can delete it.

1. **Click** on the **graphic line**. Six black handles will appear around the line.

2. **Press** the **Delete key**. The line will be deleted.

ADDING AN ARROW

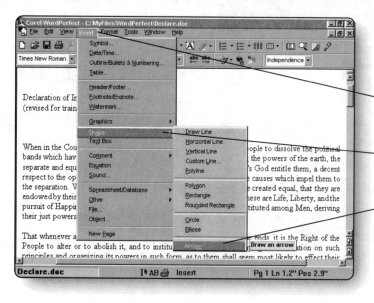

You can draw an arrow to call attention to something in your document.

1. **Click** on **Insert**. The Insert menu will appear.

2. **Click** on **Shape**. The Shape cascading menu will appear.

3. **Click** on **Arrow**. The mouse pointer will turn into a black cross.

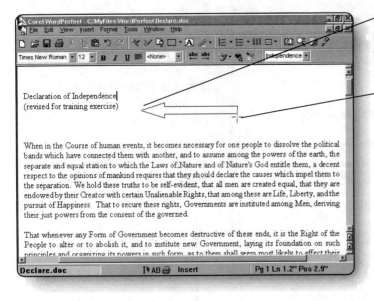

4. **Click** at the **starting point** of the arrow. This is where the arrowhead will appear.

5. **Drag** the **mouse pointer** across the area where you want the arrow to appear. The outline of your arrow appears as you are dragging the mouse.

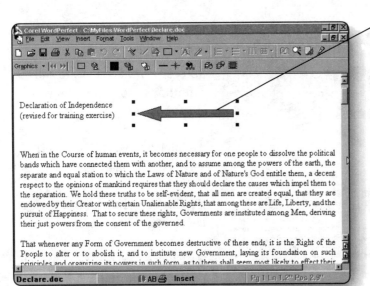

6. **Release** the **mouse button**. An arrow will be inserted in your document.

NOTE

The arrow can be selected, moved, sized, or deleted in the same manner as a graphic line.

23 Working with Graphic Images

More than 12,000 clip art images and 250 photos are provided with WordPerfect. However, during a standard installation, only some of these are copied to your hard drive. Most of these clip art images are stored on the Corel WordPerfect Suite CD. In this chapter, you'll learn how to:

✦ Add, resize, and move a graphic image

✦ Change the border of a graphic image

✦ Wrap text around a graphic image

ADDING A GRAPHIC IMAGE

You can insert many types of graphic images into your document. WordPerfect can automatically convert and read images in many standard formats, including .wpg, .wmf, .jpg, .gif, .tif, .bmp, and .pcx.

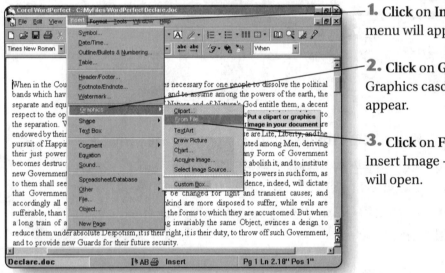

1. **Click** on **Insert**. The Insert menu will appear.

2. **Click** on **Graphics**. The Graphics cascading menu will appear.

3. **Click** on **From File**. The Insert Image - ClipArt dialog box will open.

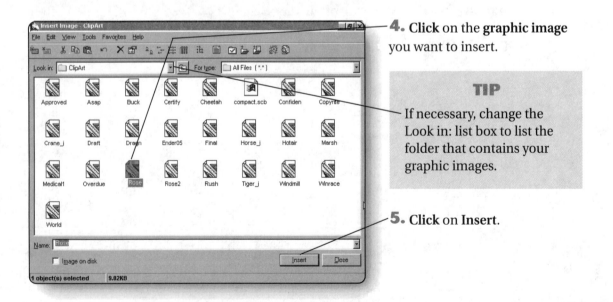

4. **Click** on the **graphic image** you want to insert.

TIP

If necessary, change the Look in: list box to list the folder that contains your graphic images.

5. **Click** on **Insert**.

The graphic image will be inserted into your document.

The Property Bar will reflect graphic image choices.

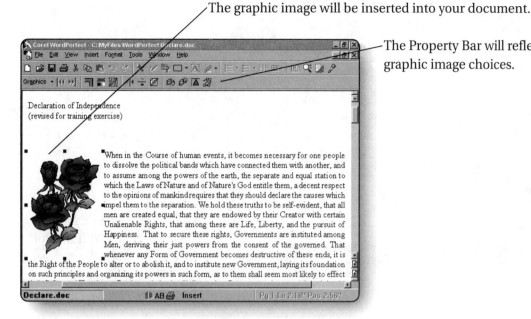

RESIZING A GRAPHIC IMAGE

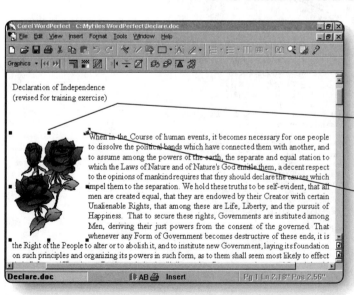

When you resize a graphic image, you are not really resizing the graphic itself—just the boundaries that surround it.

1. **Click** on the **graphic**. Eight small sizing handles will appear around the image.

2. **Position** the **mouse pointer** on one of the sizing handles. The mouse pointer will turn into a double-headed arrow.

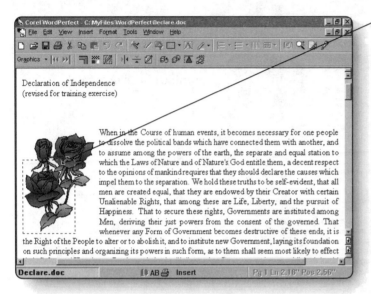

3. **Drag** the **sizing handle** to change the size of the graphic box. A dotted box will show the new size of the box.

TIP

Be sure to place the mouse pointer directly on a handle when you drag. If you use the corner handles to resize a box, the size of the box adjusts to preserve the current height-width ratio of the box and keep the original proportions of the image.

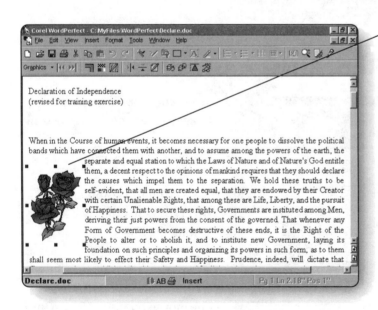

4. **Release** the **mouse button**. The graphic image will be resized.

MOVING A GRAPHIC IMAGE

The graphic image can be moved to any position on your page.

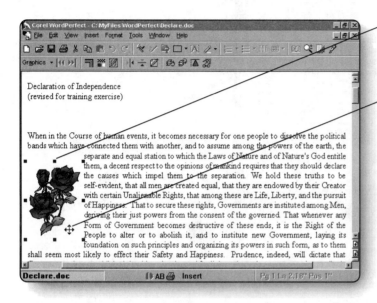

1. Click on the **graphic**. Eight small sizing handles will appear around the image.

2. Position the **mouse pointer** anywhere on the graphic box *except* on any of the sizing handles. The mouse pointer will turn into a black cross with four arrowheads.

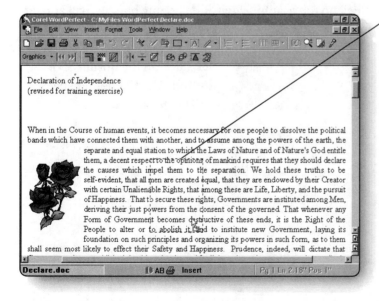

3. Click and **drag** the **graphic** to a new location. A dotted box will show where the graphic will be placed.

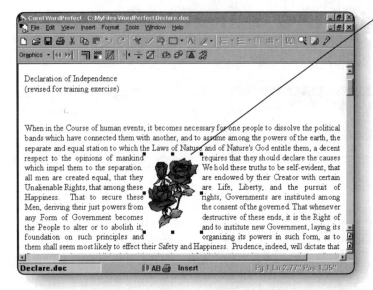

4. **Release** the **mouse button**. The graphic will be moved to the new location.

CHANGING THE BORDER OF A GRAPHIC IMAGE

The graphic box does not have a border around it, but there are over 30 different styles of borders you can apply to your graphic image.

1. **Click** on the **graphic**. Eight small sizing handles will appear around the image.

2. **Click** on the **Border Style button**. A box of border styles will be displayed.

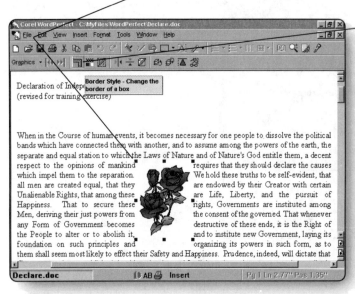

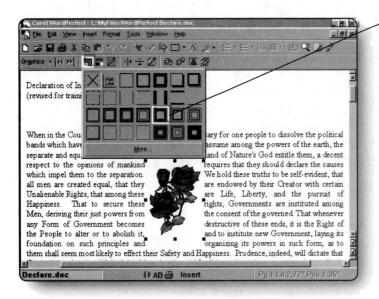

3. **Click** on the desired **border style**. The selection box will close.

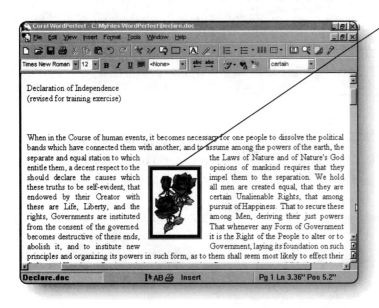

The selected border will be applied to your graphic image.

WRAPPING TEXT AROUND A GRAPHIC IMAGE

By default, the text will appear on both sides of a graphic image. There are several selections available for the wrapping of text, including contouring. Contouring text eliminates the extra white space around a graphic. Any borders are removed and the text will wrap around the image.

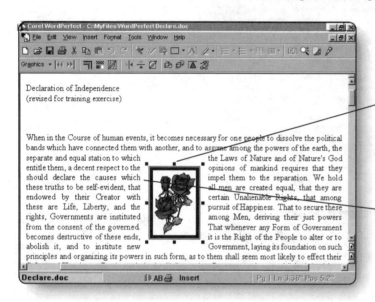

1. **Click** on the **graphic**. Eight small sizing handles will appear around the image.

> ### NOTE
>
> Notice how the text appears on both sides of the graphic and follows the rectangular outline of the box.

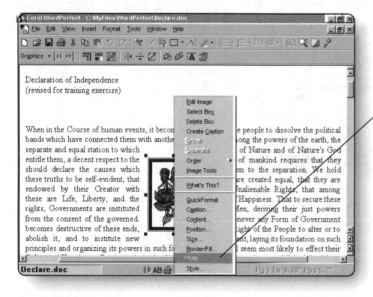

2. **Click** on the **right mouse button** on top of the graphic image. A shortcut menu will appear.

3. **Click** on **Wrap**. The Wrap Text dialog box will open.

4. **Click** on a **Wrapping Type**. This determines the shape the text will take around the graphic image.

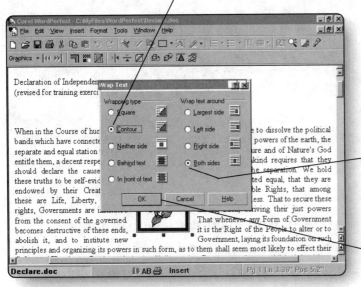

5. **Click** on a **selection** from the Wrap text around area. This will designate the placement of the text next to the graphic.

6. **Click** on **OK**. The Wrap Text dialog box will close.

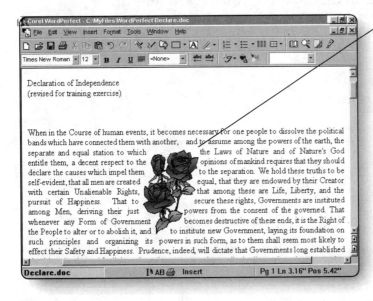

The text will be contoured around the graphic. Any border previously placed around the image will disappear.

24 Working with TextArt

TextArt is used to change words in your documents into graphic designs. You can create both two-dimensional and three-dimensional TextArt shapes. The image can be molded from a wide variety of interesting shapes and modified more using patterns, colors, and other options. In this chapter, you'll learn how to:

✦ **Create TextArt text**

✦ **Change TextArt shapes**

✦ **Change 2-D and 3-D options**

CREATING TEXTART TEXT

TextArt's special effects can be applied to text you have already typed in your document.

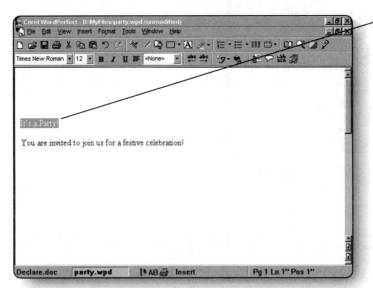

1. **Select** the **text** to be converted to a TextArt object.

NOTE

Use short lines of text, if possible. Too much text in a TextArt graphic box is hard to read.

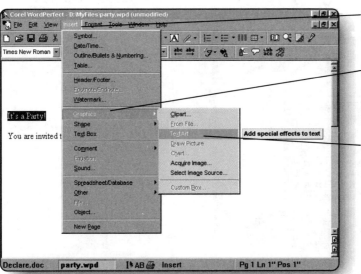

2. **Click** on **Insert**. The Insert menu will appear.

3. **Click** on **Graphics**. The Graphics cascading menu will appear.

4. **Click** on **TextArt**. The Corel TextArt 8.0 dialog box will open.

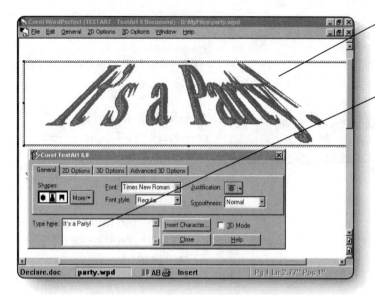

After a short time, your selected text appears in a predefined TextArt shape.

5. Optionally, **type** in **different text** in the Type here: box.

CHANGING TEXTART SHAPES

There are 57 possible shapes for your text.

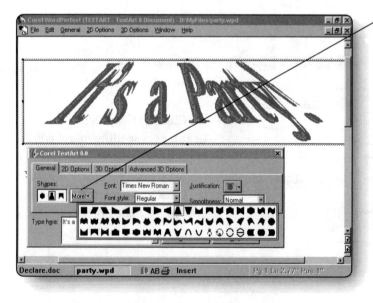

1. **Click** on the **More button**. The additional shapes box will appear.

2. **Click** on the **shape** you want for your text. Click on the various shapes and watch your text change.

3. **Click** on the **down arrow** (▼) next to the Font: list box. A list of available fonts will appear. Your font choices may vary from the ones you see in this figure.

4. **Click** on a **font** for your text. Your TextArt will reflect the newly selected font.

5. Click on the **down arrow** (▼) next to the Font style: list box to see the available style choices for the font you selected earlier.

6. Click on a **font style** such as bold or italics. The new style will be applied to your TextArt.

7. Click on the **Justification button** to see your alignment choices.

8. Click on an **alignment** for the text such as left-, center-, or right-aligned. The TextArt will be aligned as you selected.

CHANGING 2-D OPTIONS

Two-dimensional options will include choices such as color or pattern of your text.

1. Click on the **2D Options tab.** The tab will come to the top of the stack.

2. Click on the **Preset button** to display five predefined color and shape options.

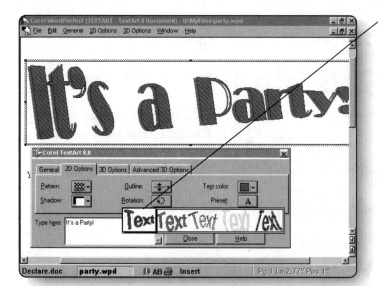

Go Ahead! Experiment with these choices!

3. **Click** on the **Text Color button**. A list of available color options will appear.

4. **Click** on the **color** you want for your text.

5. **Click** on the **Pattern button**. Twenty-four different pattern possibilities for your text will appear.

6. **Click** on a **Pattern**.

7. Optionally, **change** the text pattern **background color**.

8. **Click** on **OK**. The pattern box will close.

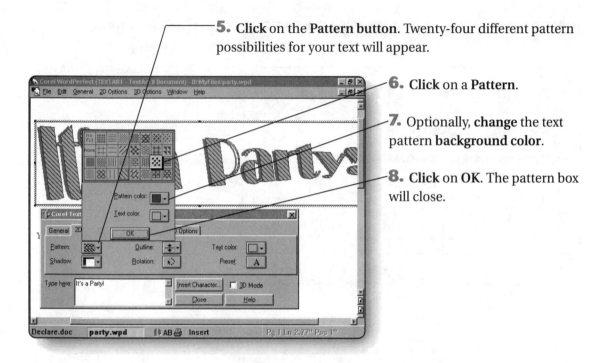

Your text will be modified to the pattern you selected.

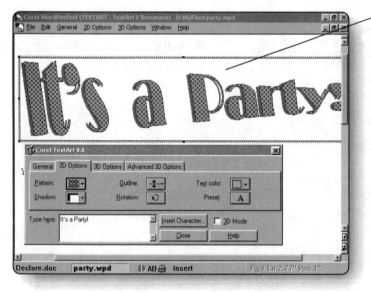

CHANGING 3-D OPTIONS

For even more design, add a three-dimensional effect to your text!

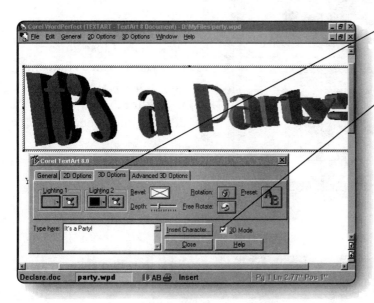

1. **Click** on the **3D Options tab**. The tab will come to the top of the stack.

2. **Click** on **3D Mode** to activate three-dimensional options. Your text will be automatically converted to a three-dimensional shape.

> **NOTE**
>
> Adding three-dimensional effects to TextArt will substantially increase the size of your file. As an example, a file that started as 2K in size is increased to 26K when a two-dimensional TextArt object is added, and then to 277K when a three-dimensional object is added.

3. **Click** on the **Preset button** to select from the 15 predefined color and shape options.

To add even more effects you can increase or decrease the bevel depth of the three-dimensional text.

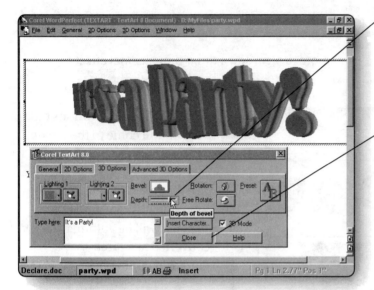

4. **Click** and **drag** the **Depth: slide bar** to the left to decrease the depth of the characters or to the right to increase the depth of the characters.

5. **Click** on the **Close button** when you are finished changing options for the TextArt object. You will return to your WordPerfect document.

6. **Click anywhere** outside the TextArt box to deselect the graphic object.

TIP

To further edit the TextArt object, double-click on the TextArt object. The Corel TextArt 8.0 box will reopen.

A TextArt object is like any of the other graphic objects you have worked with. It can be resized, moved, or deleted as covered in Chapter 22. You can also add borders to it or change the way text wraps around it as covered in Chapter 23.

PART V REVIEW QUESTIONS

1.   What type of line runs from left margin to right margin? *See "Adding a Graphic Line" in Chapter 22*

2.   What should the mouse pointer look like before you select a graphic line? *See "Moving a Graphic Line" in Chapter 22*

3.   After selecting a graphic line, what key do you press to delete it? *See "Deleting a Graphic Line" in Chapter 22*

4.   Does the arrowhead appear at the beginning or end of an arrow as you draw it? *See "Adding an Arrow" in Chapter 22*

5.   To resize a graphic box, should the mouse pointer be on a handle or on the border line of the graphic? *See "Resizing a Graphic Image" in Chapter 23*

6.   What does contouring text do to the graphic? *See "Wrapping Text around a Graphic Image" in Chapter 23*

7.   Why should you use short lines of text when creating a TextArt object? *See "Creating TextArt Text" in Chapter 24*

8.   What does clicking on the Preset button do? *See "Changing TextArt Shapes" in Chapter 24*

9.   Which TextArt file will be larger—a two-dimensional or a three-dimensional one? *See "Changing 3-D Options" in Chapter 24*

10.   If a TextArt object has been deselected in a WordPerfect document, what must you do to further edit the object? *See "Changing 3-D Options" in Chapter 24*

PART VI

Working on the Internet

25 Using QuickLinks

With the QuickLink feature you can automatically create hyperlinks when you type certain kinds of text. For example, when you type text that begins with "www," "ftp," "http," or "mailto," QuickLinks will automatically convert it to an Internet link. In this chapter, you'll learn how to:

✦ Create and edit a QuickLink

✦ Add a QuickLink in a document

✦ Use a QuickLink

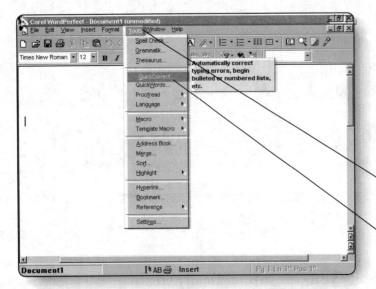

CREATING A QUICKLINK

Use QuickLinks to set up frequently used Internet links or even links to other WordPerfect documents.

1. **Click** on **Tools**. The Tools menu will appear.

2. **Click** on **QuickCorrect**. The QuickCorrect dialog box will open.

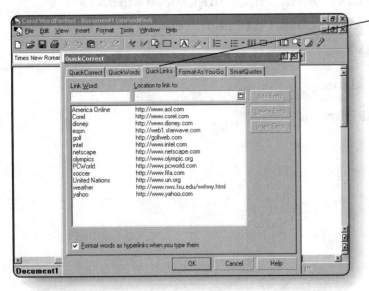

3. **Click** on the **QuickLinks tab**. The tab will come to the top of the stack. WordPerfect has already included several QuickLinks for you to use.

4. Type the **word** you want to type in your document to create a link in the Link Word: text box.

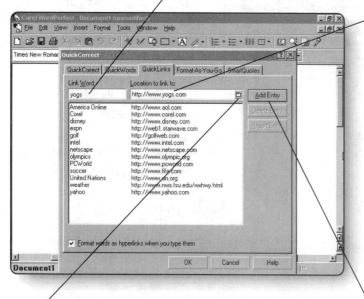

5. Type the **actual address** in the Location to link to: text box. This could be an Internet address or a document address.

For example, you could specify that typing the word "Corel" automatically sets up a link to the Corel Home Page at http://www.corel.com or perhaps typing the words Sales Report creates a link to a WordPerfect document called C:\MyFiles\Sales Report.wpd.

6. Click on the **Add Entry button**.

TIP

Click on the Browse folder to look for a specific file to link to.

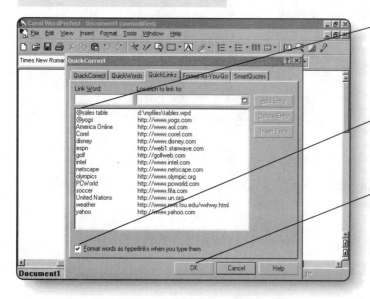

The entry will be added to the existing list, with the @ character inserted at the beginning of the Link Word.

Make sure that Format words as hyperlinks when you type them is turned on.

7. Click on **OK**. The dialog box will close.

You are now ready to insert a QuickLink into your document.

EDITING A QUICKLINK

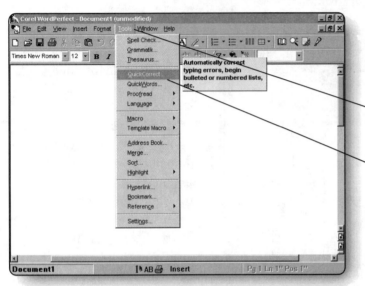

If the Web address or document you created a link to changes, you will need to change the QuickLink.

1. **Click** on **Tools**. The Tools menu will appear.

2. **Click** on **QuickCorrect**. The QuickCorrect dialog box will open.

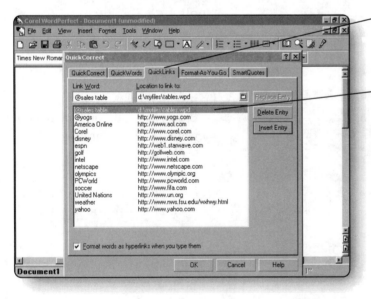

3. **Click** on the **QuickLinks tab**. The tab will come to the top of the stack.

4. **Click** on the **link** to be changed. The current information will appear in the Link Word: and Location to link to: text boxes.

5. **Make** any necessary **changes** in either the Link Word: or the Location to link to: text boxes.

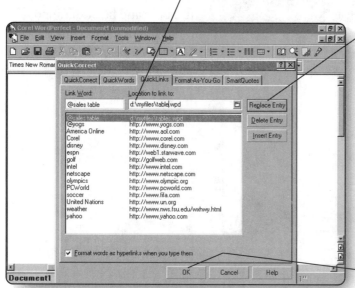

6. **Click** on the **Replace Entry button**. The QuickLink will be modified.

NOTE

To delete a QuickLink, click on the entry to be deleted, and then click on the Delete Entry button. You will be asked to confirm the deletion.

7. **Click** on **OK**. The QuickLink dialog box will close.

ADDING A QUICKLINK TO A DOCUMENT

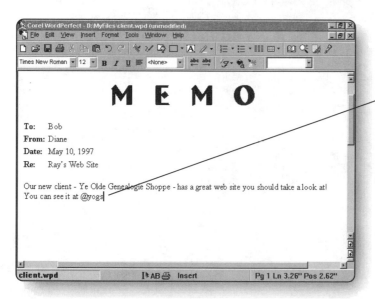

1. **Position** the **insertion point** in the document where the link is to be created.

2. **Type** the **Link Word** you created. Be sure to include the @ symbol at the beginning.

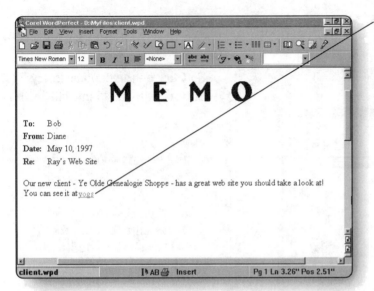

3. **Press** the **spacebar** or the **Enter key**. The Link Word will turn blue and be underlined, indicating that it is a link to the location you specified. The @ symbol will be removed.

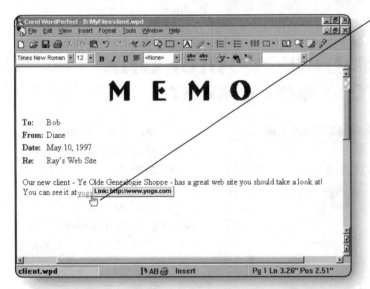

4. **Position** the **mouse pointer** on top of the link. The mouse pointer will turn into a small hand and the actual location of the link will be specified in a pop-up box.

USING A QUICKLINK

Use a QuickLink to quickly jump to another document or Web site.

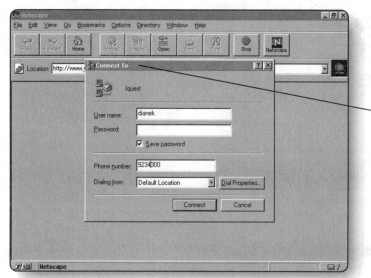

1. **Click** on the **QuickLink**.

Several things could happen at this point:

✦ If the link is an Internet link and you are not yet connected to the Internet, WordPerfect will first launch your Internet browser and attempt to launch a connection. It will then jump to the link location.

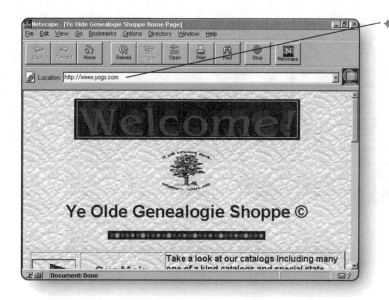

✦ If the link is an Internet link and you are already connected to the Internet, WordPerfect will launch your Internet browser program and jump to the link location.

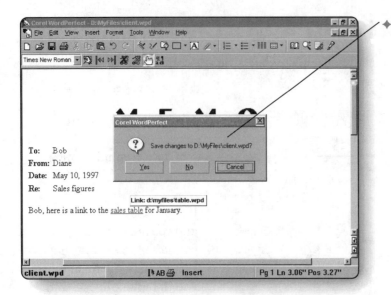

✦ If the link is to another WordPerfect document, you will be prompted to save the current document, if necessary.

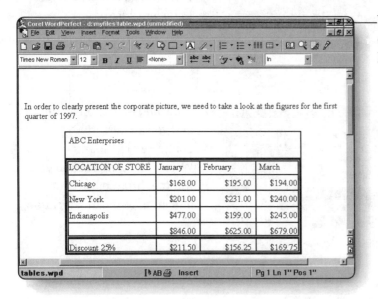

WordPerfect will then close the current document and open the linked one.

26 Creating a Simple Web Page

In the not so very distant past, to create a Web page you had to learn a type of programming language called HTML (Hypertext Markup Language). WordPerfect has eliminated the need to learn HTML by having the ability to convert regular text on the screen to the HTML code for us. You can now create Web pages by simply creating a WordPerfect document. In this chapter, you'll learn how to:

✦ **Start the PerfectExpert**

✦ **Change the background color and wallpaper of a Web page**

✦ **Add text and a graphic image to a Web page**

✦ **Publish to HTML**

✦ **View the HTML document in a Web browser**

STARTING THE PERFECTEXPERT

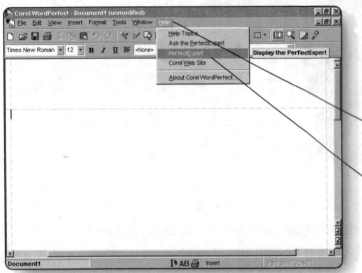

WordPerfect has a PerfectExpert to assist you in designing your own Web Page but it will work best if you begin with a blank document on your screen.

1. **Click** on **Help**. The Help menu will appear.

2. **Click** on **PerfectExpert**. The PerfectExpert window will appear on the left side of your screen.

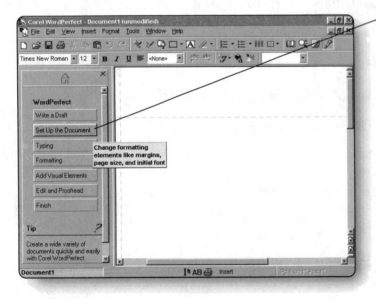

3. **Click** on the **Set Up the Document button**. A new selection of choices appear in the PerfectExpert window.

You may or may not be informed that you can click on the PerfectExpert Home button to return to the initial PerfectExpert screen.

4. If you do receive this message, **click** on **OK** to acknowledge it.

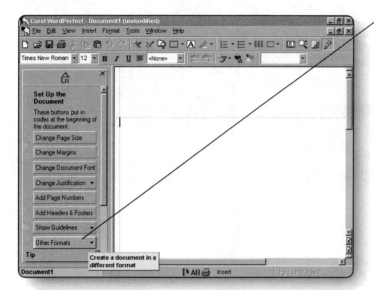

5. **Click** on **Other Formats**. A list of available format choices will appear.

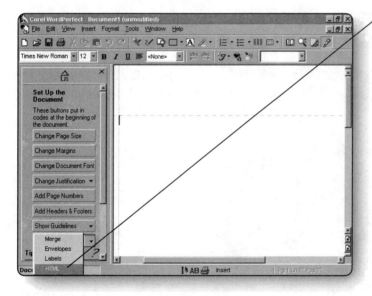

6. **Click** on **HTML**. This is the format of document you must use to create a Web Page.

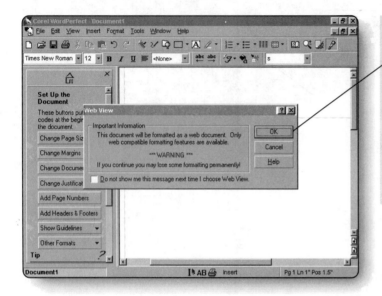

If you did not start with a blank screen at the beginning you will get a formatting warning message advising you that you may lose some formatting already in place. Click on OK to continue.

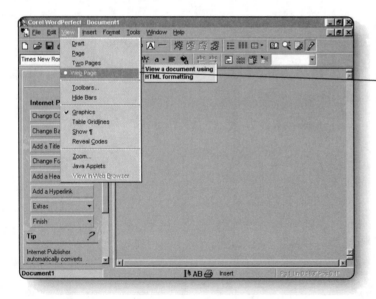

A blank Web page will appear on your screen.

Your view will automatically change to Web Page view.

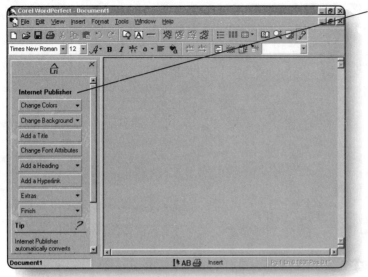

The PerfectExpert will change to the Internet Publisher PerfectExpert.

CHANGING THE COLORS OF A WEB PAGE

By default, the background of a Web page is gray with black text. WordPerfect has plenty of color combinations predesigned for you or you can create your own combination.

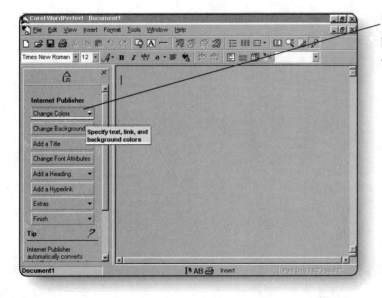

1. **Click** on the **Change Colors button**. A color choice menu will appear.

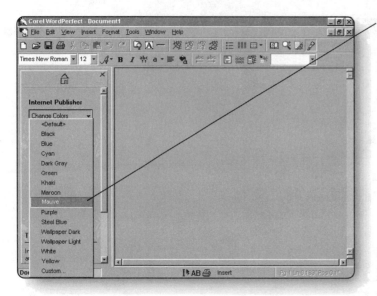

2. Click on the **background color** of your choice. The blank document screen will automatically update to your background color selection.

CHANGING THE WALLPAPER OF A WEB PAGE

Instead of a plain solid color background, try one of the many wallpapers WordPerfect supplies. There are wallpapers that look like fabrics, wood, stones, and many other categories.

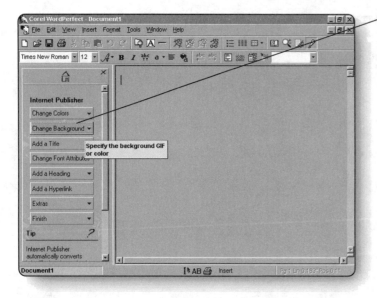

1. Click on the **Change Background button**. A sample selection of background patterns will appear.

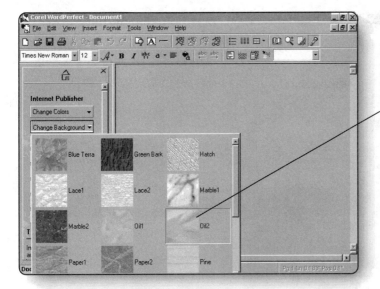

There are over 350 backgrounds in nine different categories from which to choose, however only a few are displayed here.

2a. Click on the **background wallpaper** you want for your Web page.

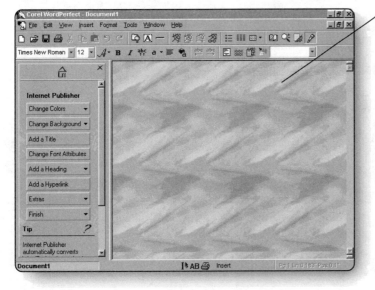

The wallpaper will be displayed in your document.

OR

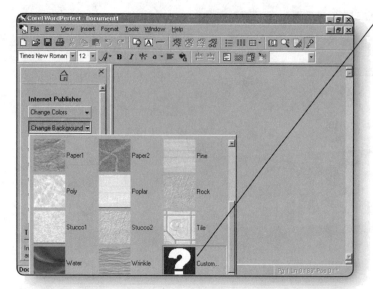

2b. **Scroll** to the **bottom** of the samples and **click** on **Custom**. The HTML Document Properties dialog box will open.

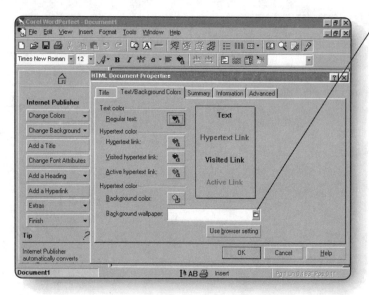

3. **Click** on the **Background wallpaper Browse button** to choose a different wallpaper.

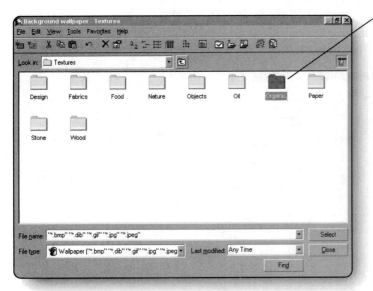

4. Double-click on the **folder** that contains the category you want for your background. The folder will open and display a list of wallpaper choices.

5. Click on the **filename** of the wallpaper you want to use.

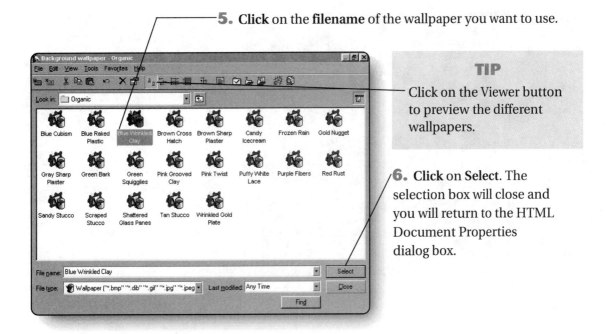

6. Click on **Select**. The selection box will close and you will return to the HTML Document Properties dialog box.

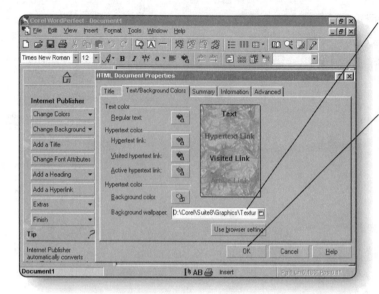

The name and path of your selection has been inserted into the Background wallpaper: text box.

7. **Click** on **OK.** The HTML Document Properties dialog box will close.

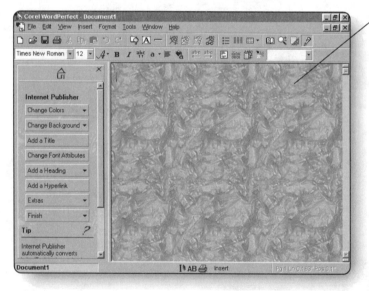

The wallpaper will be displayed in your document.

FORMATTING TEXT ON A WEB PAGE

Adding text to a Web page is the same as typing in any WordPerfect document, however not quite as many formatting choices are available in an HTML document as in a standard WordPerfect document.

1. **Type** the desired **text** just like you would in a regular WordPerfect document.

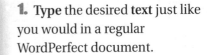
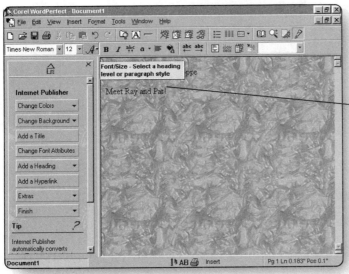

2. **Click** in the **paragraph** to be formatted.

3. **Click** on the **Font/Size button** on the HTML toolbar. A list of available styles will appear showing you a sample of each style.

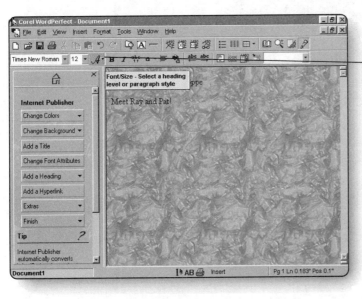

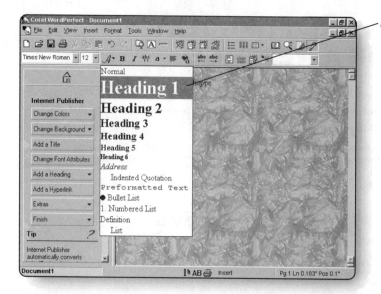

4. **Click** on a **style** for your text.

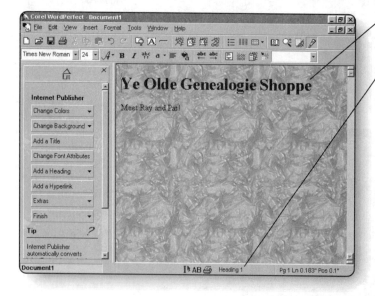

The paragraph is changed to the new size/style.

The current paragraph style is reflected in the status bar.

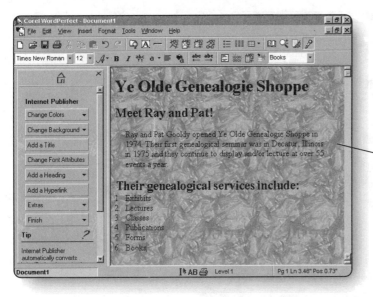

5. **Continue typing** any additional text in the Web page document.

6. **Format** as advised in **steps 3** through **5** above.

A sample Web page is shown with several different styles applied.

ADDING A GRAPHIC IMAGE TO A WEB PAGE

HTML documents only support .gif or .jpg graphic images, however you can insert graphics in any format WordPerfect supports. The graphics are converted to .gif or .jpg images automatically when you save the document to HTML. You can also add horizontal lines to separate sections of an HTML document.

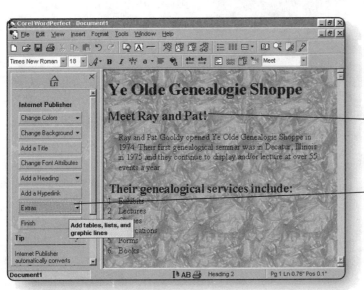

1. **Position** the **insertion point** at the location where you want the graphic to appear.

2. **Click** on the **Extras button** on the PerfectExpert window. A list of additional Web page features will appear.

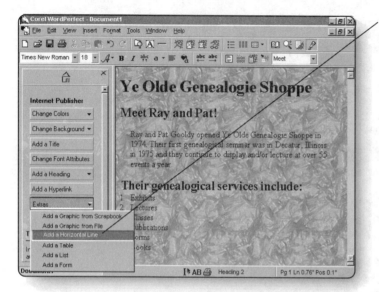

3. Click on **Add a Horizontal Line**.

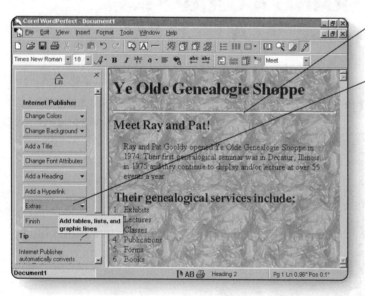

A horizontal line will be inserted into the document.

4. Click on the **Extras button** on the PerfectExpert window. A list of additional Web page features will appear.

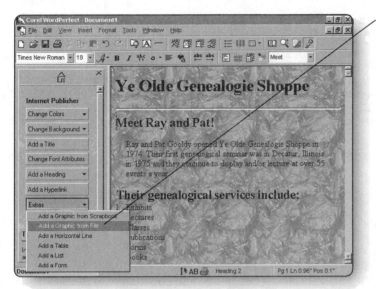

5. **Click** on **Add a Graphic from File**. The Insert Image - ClipArt dialog box will open.

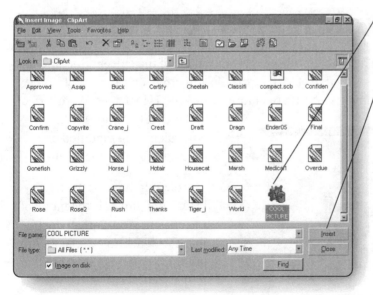

6. **Click** on the **graphic** you want to appear on your Web page document.

7. **Click** on **Insert**. The dialog box will close.

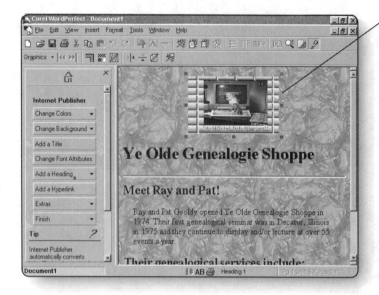

The graphic will be inserted into your document.

PUBLISHING TO HTML

When you publish to HTML, a copy of the current document is recreated in HTML format. WordPerfect automatically converts WordPerfect formatting into HTML tags. WordPerfect codes that have no HTML equivalents are modified or deleted from the document.

The default name of the new HTML document is the name of the current WordPerfect document with a .htm extension. Any graphic images are saved in the folder you specify.

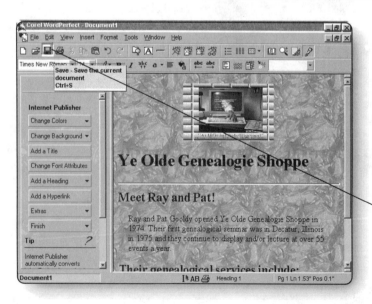

1. **Click** on the **Save button** to save your document as you would any other WordPerfect document. The Save As dialog box will open.

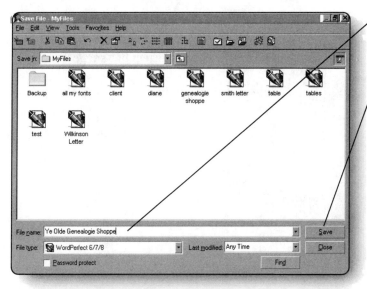

2. **Type** a **name** for your document in the File name: list box.

3. **Click** on **Save**. The document will be saved in a WordPerfect format.

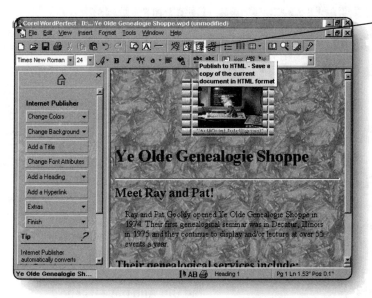

4. **Click** on the **Publish to HTML button**. The Publish to HTML dialog box will open.

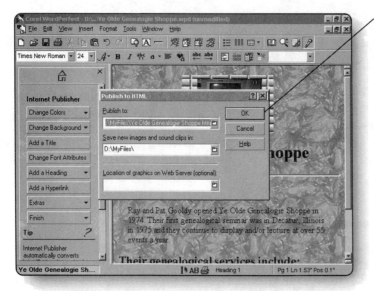

5. **Click** on **OK** to save the document with the settings WordPerfect has suggested.

You will see a box briefly appear advising you that WordPerfect is converting your file.

VIEWING THE HTML DOCUMENT IN A WEB BROWSER

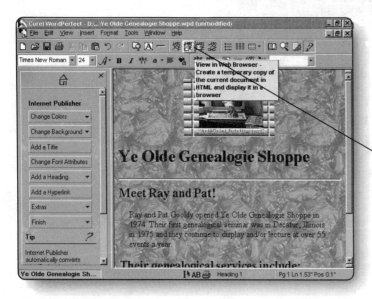

How you see the document in the WordPerfect window is not necessarily how it will appear in a Web browser such as Netscape Navigator or Microsoft Internet Explorer.

1. **Click** on the **View in Web Browser button**. WordPerfect will launch your default browser and the Web page will be displayed.

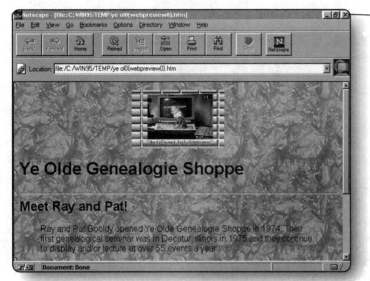

2. **Click** on the **Close button** of the Web browser to return to your WordPerfect document.

TIP

HTML documents will look different in different Web browsers, even between different versions of the same Web browser. Try to view your HTML document in as many different browsers as possible.

27 Getting Help

Although I sincerely hope you find many answers to your WordPerfect questions from this book, sometimes you need additional information. WordPerfect supplies you with several types of assistance. In this chapter, you'll learn how to:

✦ Get PerfectExpert help

✦ Use Help Topics

✦ Use Help Online

GETTING PERFECTEXPERT HELP

Get the expert assistance you need from the PerfectExpert!

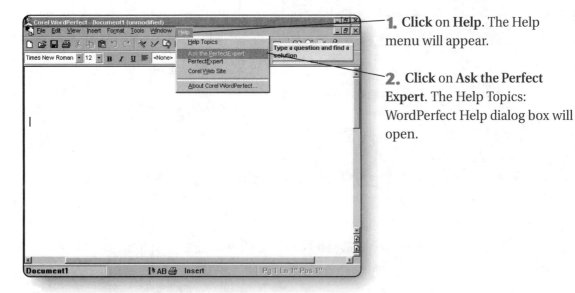

1. Click on **Help**. The Help menu will appear.

2. Click on **Ask the Perfect Expert**. The Help Topics: WordPerfect Help dialog box will open.

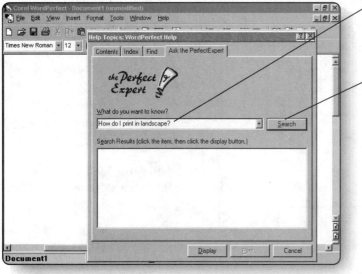

3. Type your **question** in the "What do you want to know?" list box.

4. Click on **Search**.

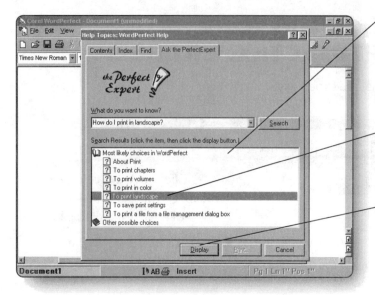

WordPerfect will search for any topic that might be closely related to your question and display the results in the Search Results box.

5. **Click** on the **choice** that most closely resembles the issue you are seeking.

6. **Click** on **Display**.

A yellow Help window will appear with step-by-step instructions for the feature you asked about.

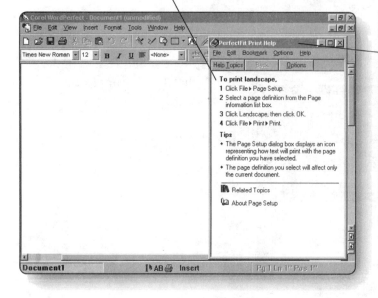

NOTE

The title of the Help window will vary depending upon the question you asked. It may say WordPerfect Help, PerfectFit Print Help, PerfectFit Browser Help, or a number of other choices.

You can print a paper copy of the Help instructions.

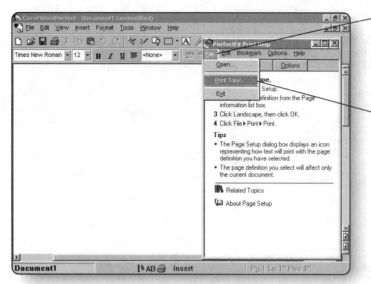

7. Click on the **Help window File menu**. (Be sure to choose File on the Help window, not your document window!)

8. Click on **Print Topic**. The Print dialog box will open.

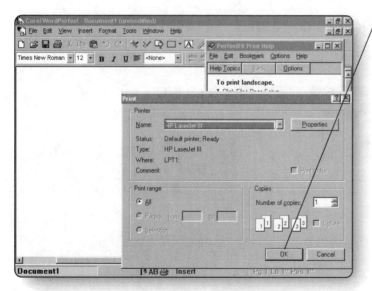

9. Click on **OK**. The topic will be printed out for you.

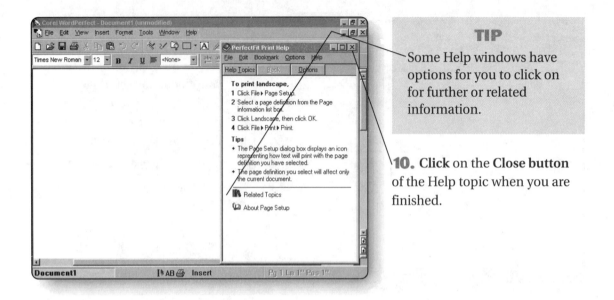

Some Help windows have options for you to click on for further or related information.

10. **Click** on the **Close button** of the Help topic when you are finished.

USING HELP TOPICS

Help Topics is an index of all WordPerfect features.

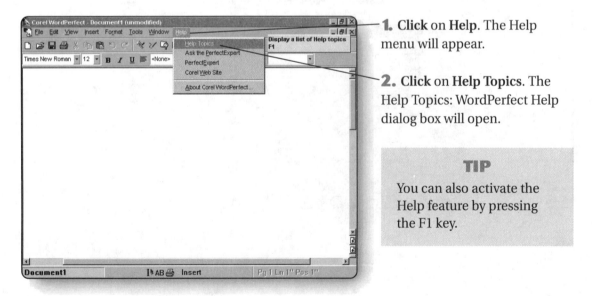

1. **Click** on **Help**. The Help menu will appear.

2. **Click** on **Help Topics**. The Help Topics: WordPerfect Help dialog box will open.

You can also activate the Help feature by pressing the F1 key.

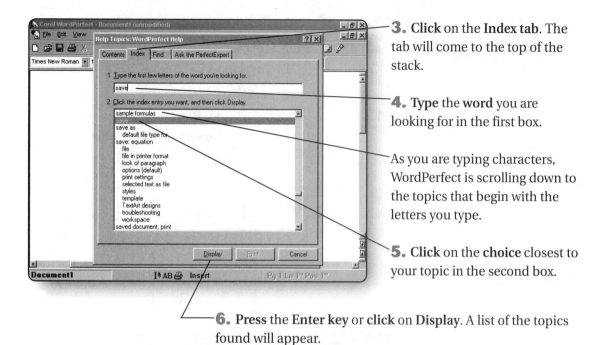

3. **Click** on the **Index tab**. The tab will come to the top of the stack.

4. **Type** the **word** you are looking for in the first box.

As you are typing characters, WordPerfect is scrolling down to the topics that begin with the letters you type.

5. **Click** on the **choice** closest to your topic in the second box.

6. **Press** the **Enter key** or **click** on **Display**. A list of the topics found will appear.

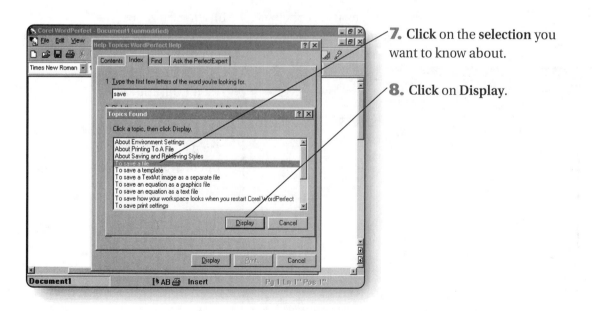

7. **Click** on the **selection** you want to know about.

8. **Click** on **Display**.

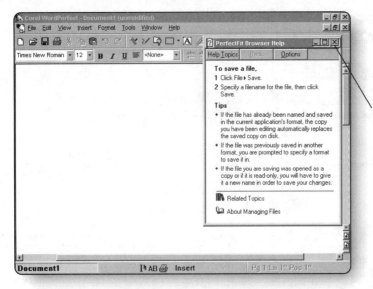

A yellow Help window will appear with step-by-step instructions for the feature for which you searched.

9. **Click** on the **Close button** of the Help window when you are finished.

USING HELP ONLINE

You can also get help via the Internet from the Corel WordPerfect 8 Home Page.

1. **Click** on **Help**. The Help menu will appear.

2. **Click** on **Corel Web Site**. The Help Online dialog box may open, prompting you to select a service.

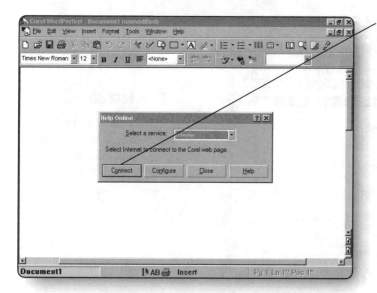

3. Click on the **Connect button**.

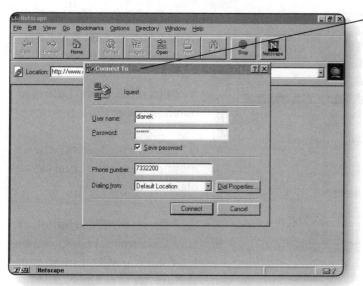

Your Web browser will launch and if necessary, you will be connected to your Internet Service Provider.

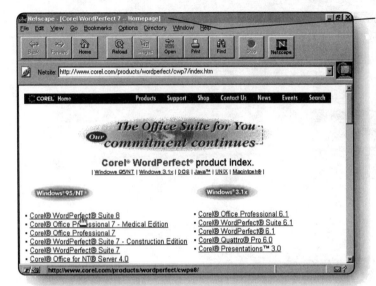

After your connection is made, the Corel WordPerfect Home Page will appear.

NOTE

Web pages are continually being updated. Your screen may not look exactly like the one in these figures.

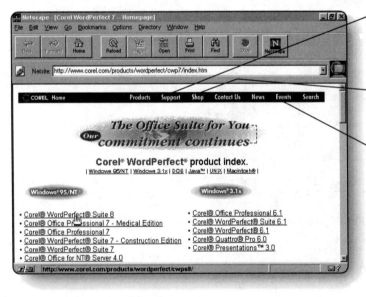

4. Click on the **Support button** to see Corel's available options for WordPerfect support.

5. Click on the **Shop button** to purchase other Corel products.

6. Click on the **Events button** to monitor upcoming Corel events planned for your city.

7. Click on the **Close button** of your Web browser when you are finished. You will return to your WordPerfect document.

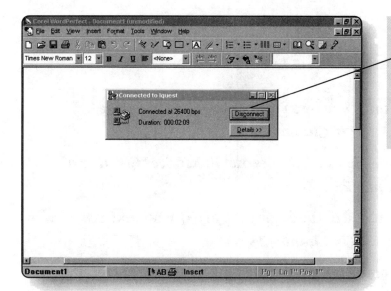

NOTE

Depending on the type of connection you have to the Internet, you may also need to disconnect from the Service Provider as well.

PART VI REVIEW QUESTIONS

1. **Which dialog box must you open to access QuickLinks?** *See "Creating a QuickLink" in Chapter 25*

2. **Can QuickLinks only be used for Internet links?** *See "Creating a QuickLink" in Chapter 25*

3. **What character is added to the beginning of a QuickLink?** *See "Creating a QuickLink" in Chapter 25*

4. **What is the name of the programming language used in creating Web pages?** *See "Creating a Simple Web Page" in Chapter 26*

5. **What view does WordPerfect display when creating a Web page?** *See "Starting the PerfectExpert" in Chapter 26*

6. **How many categories of backgrounds does WordPerfect supply?** *See "Changing the Wallpaper of a Web Page" in Chapter 26*

7. **What two formats of graphic images can an HTML document support?** *See" Adding a Graphic Image to a Web Page" in Chapter 26*

8. **Why should you try to view your HTML document in as many different Web Browsers as possible?** *See "Viewing the HTML Document in a Web Browser" in Chapter 26*

9. **What key can you press to activate the Help feature?** *See "Using Help Topics" in Chapter 27*

10. **While at the Corel WordPerfect Web site, what button should you click to access information on upcoming Corel events?** *See "Using Help Online" in Chapter 27*

PART VII
Appendixes

A
Creating an Event Calendar

WordPerfect has a built-in monthly calendar for you to track your events. With the help of WordPerfect's PerfectExpert, you can even add clip art to show those "special days." In this appendix, you'll learn how to:

✦ **Create the calendar**

✦ **Add an event to the calendar**

✦ **Add a graphic to the calendar**

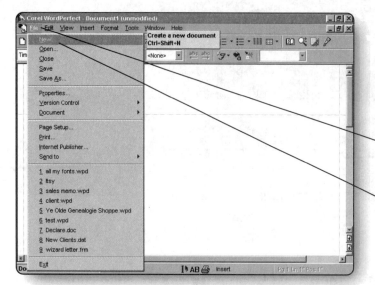

CREATING THE CALENDAR

There is a PerfectExpert to assist you with calendar creation.

1. Click on **File**. The File menu will appear.

2. Click on **New**. The New dialog box will open.

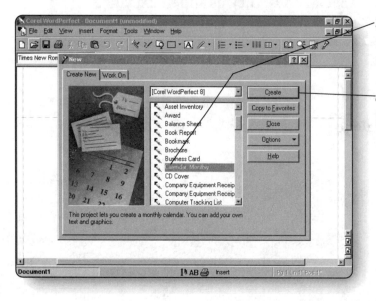

3. Click on **Calendar**. This choice creates a table showing the days of a month.

4. Click on **Create**. The dialog box will close.

A macro will start to execute.

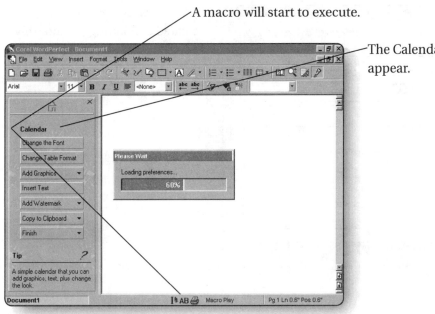

The Calendar PerfectExpert will appear.

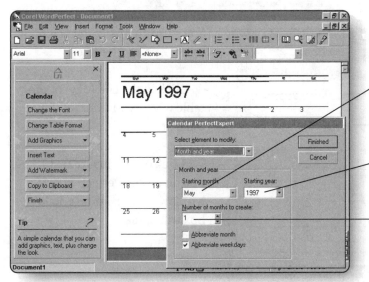

The Calendar PerfectExpert dialog box will open and prompt you for information.

5. Choose the **Starting month:** for the calendar you want to create.

6. Choose the **Starting year:** for the calendar you want to create.

7. Choose how many months you want to create. The maximum number is 12.

8. Click on **Finished** when you have made your selections from the dialog box.

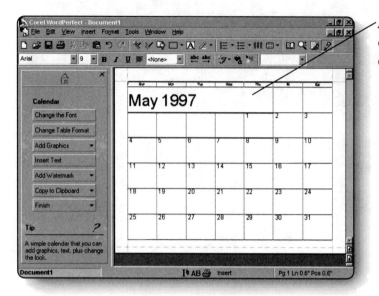

A WordPerfect table will be created containing the monthly calendar you requested.

ADDING AN EVENT TO THE CALENDAR

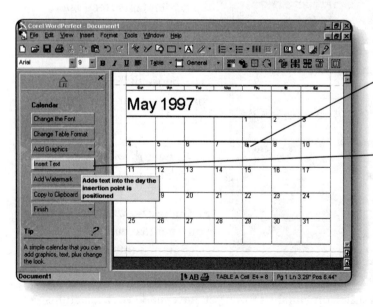

You can add text to the calendar to track your schedule.

1. **Click** in the **cell** (day) of the table where you want to add the text.

2. **Click** on the **Insert Text button** on the PerfectExpert window. The insert text dialog box will open.

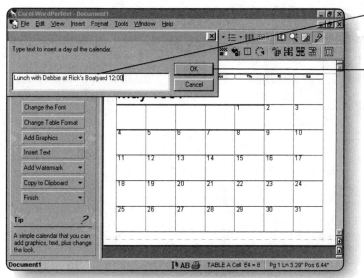

3. Type the **text** for the day's event.

4. Click on **OK**. The dialog box will close.

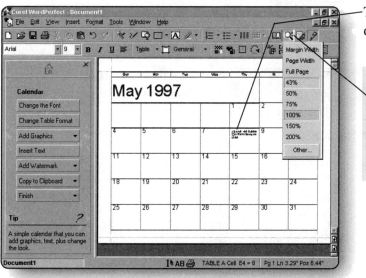

The text will be added to the calendar.

ADDING A GRAPHIC
TO THE CALENDAR

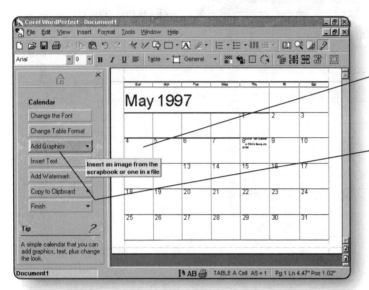

If you want to note a special day, add a graphic image to it!

1. **Click** in the **cell** (day) of the table where you want to add the graphic image.

2. **Click** on the **Add Graphics button** on the PerfectExpert window. You can add a graphic image from a disk or from the WordPerfect scrapbook.

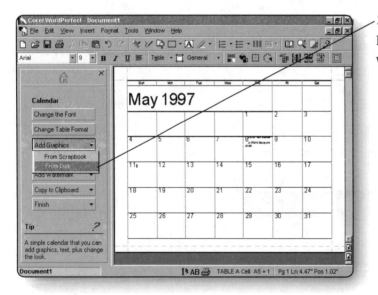

3. **Click** on **From Disk**. The Insert Image - ClipArt dialog box will open.

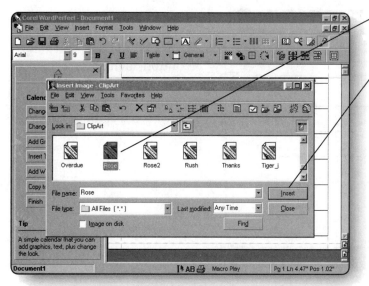

4. **Click** on the **image** you want to insert into your calendar.

5. **Click** on **Insert**. The dialog box will close.

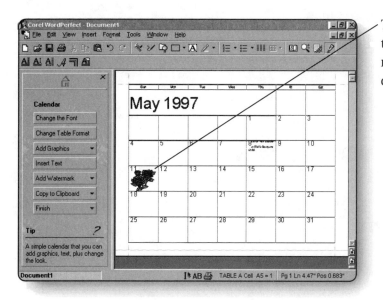

The graphic image will be added to the calendar. It can be resized, moved, or otherwise adjusted as discussed in Chapter 23.

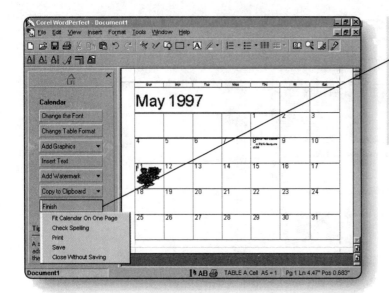

NOTE

Clicking on the Finish button opens choices to complete the calendar such as spell check, saving, or printing.

B WordPerfect Tips and Tricks

I have put together a few of my favorite hints, tips, and tricks for you. I hope you enjoy them! In this appendix, you'll learn how to:

✦ Keep two words together

✦ Look at all your fonts

✦ Add a drop cap to a paragraph

✦ Stretch a heading

KEEPING TWO WORDS TOGETHER

To prevent word wrap from splitting a phone number or hyphenated name from one line to the next, hold down the Ctrl key while you are pressing the hyphen key (-). This tells WordPerfect not to break up these two words. You can use the same feature for two words with a space between them. Instead of pressing the spacebar by itself, hold down the Ctrl key while you press the spacebar. This is called a *Hard Hyphen* or *Hard Space.*

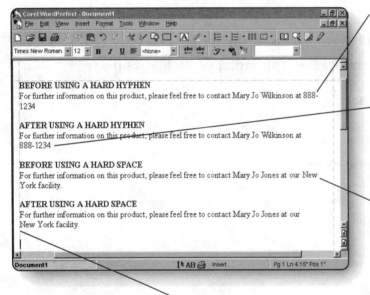

Notice how the telephone number is split between two lines by using a standard hyphen character.

After using the Ctrl key and the hyphen character at the same time, the telephone number appears on the same line.

Notice how the words "New" and "York" are on separate lines by using a standard space.

After pressing the Ctrl key and the spacebar at the same time, the words "New" and "York" are on the same line.

LOOKING AT ALL YOUR FONTS

If you are a "font junkie" like I am, you have hundreds of fonts on your system. WordPerfect has included a macro that will create a document with a sample of every font you have available.

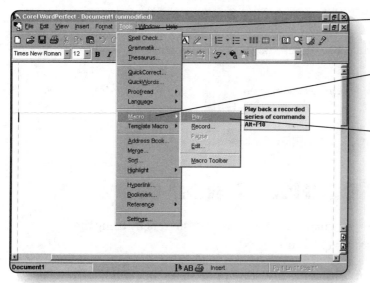

1. **Click** on **Tools**. The Tools menu will appear.

2. **Click** on **Macro**. The Macro cascading menu will appear.

3. **Click** on **Play**. The Play Macro dialog box will open.

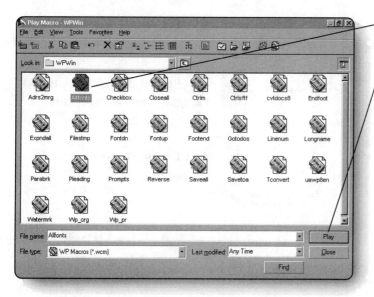

4. **Click** on the macro named "**Allfonts.**"

5. **Click** on **Play**. The macro will execute and you will see a document with sample fonts.

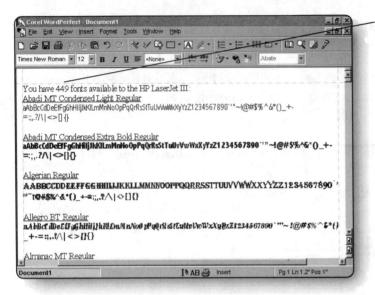

The macro tells you how many fonts you have on your system. (See, I told you I was a font junkie!)

ADDING A DROP CAP

You can really liven up your newsletters by using the Drop Cap feature.

1. Position the **insertion point** at the beginning of the paragraph to have a drop cap.

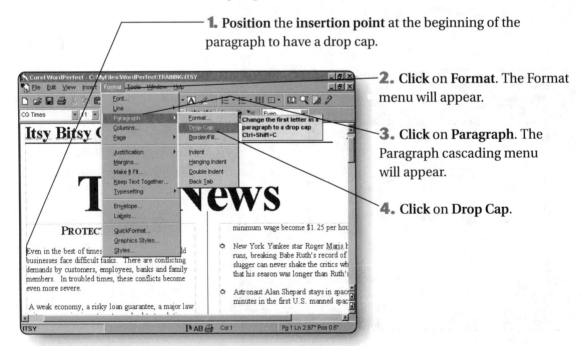

2. Click on **Format**. The Format menu will appear.

3. Click on **Paragraph**. The Paragraph cascading menu will appear.

4. Click on **Drop Cap**.

The first letter of the sentence will be converted to a drop cap— and the rest of the text will be shoved over to make room for it.

Several drop cap options appear on the Property Bar.

"STRETCHING" A HEADING

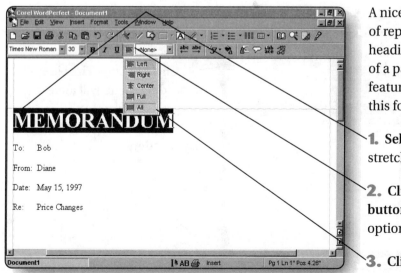

A nice effect to use for headings of reports might be to stretch the heading across the entire width of a page. WordPerfect has a feature called *justify all* to do this for you.

1. **Select** the **heading** to be stretched.

2. **Click** on the **Justification button**. A list of justification options will appear.

3. **Click** on **All**.

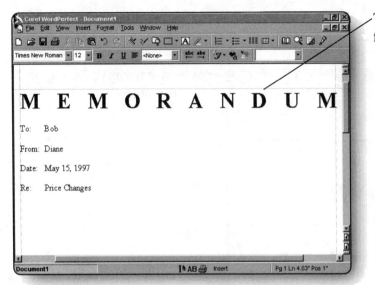

The heading will be stretched from margin to margin.

ADDING DOT LEADERS TO TEXT ON THE RIGHT MARGIN

The Flush Right with Dot Leaders feature is used to line up a portion of a line to the right margin and add dot leaders to it. This is similar to what you might see in a Table of Contents.

1. Position the **insertion point** at the portion of the line to be right-aligned.

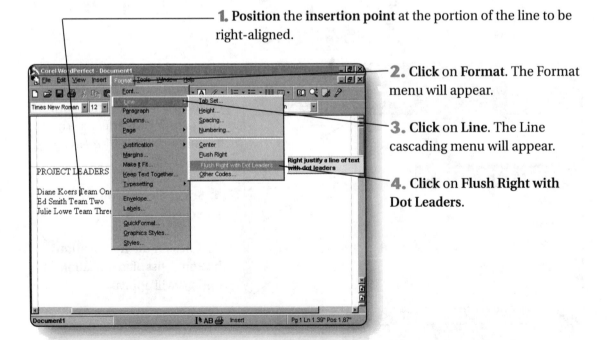

2. Click on **Format**. The Format menu will appear.

3. Click on **Line**. The Line cascading menu will appear.

4. Click on **Flush Right with Dot Leaders**.

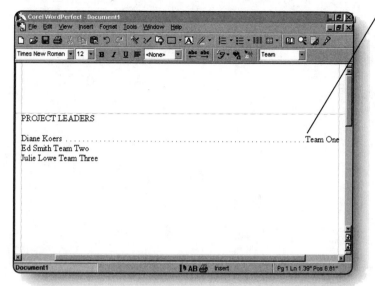

The balance of the line from the right of the insertion point will be moved to the right margin with dots leading up to it. This feature only works on one line of text at a time.

Glossary

Address Book. Stores names, addresses, and phone numbers in one handy location.

Alignment. The arrangement of text to the margins of a document or the edges of a table cell. Also called justification.

Append. To add text to the end of the Clipboard instead of replacing its contents.

Application Bar. The line at the bottom of a document window that shows information such as the page, line, and vertical and horizontal position of the insertion point. Sometimes called a Status Bar.

Attributes. Items that determine the appearance of text such as bolding, underlining, italics, or point size.

Bold. A font attribute that makes text thicker and brighter.

Bookmark. Use Bookmark to mark a place in a document so you can return to that location quickly.

Border. A line surrounding paragraphs, pages, or objects.

Bullet. A small black circle or other character that precedes each item in a list.

Cell. The intersection of a row and column in a table or spreadsheet.

Clip art. A piece of artwork inserted into a WordPerfect document.

Clipboard. An area of computer memory where text or graphics can be temporarily stored.

Close. To shut down or exit a dialog box, window, or application.

Columns. Vertical divisions of text on a page.

Comment. To add annotations to a document. Comments do not print with the document.

Copy. To take a selection from the document and duplicate it on the Clipboard.

Cut. To take a selection from the document and move it to the Clipboard.

Data file. A file that stores a collection of information called records with individual pieces of information called fields. Used in the Mail Merge process with a form file.

Default. A setting or action predetermined by the program unless changed by the user.

Desktop. The screen background and main area of Windows where you can open and manage files and programs.

Dialog box. A box that appears and lets you select options, or displays warnings and messages.

Document. A letter, memo, proposal, or other file that is created in WordPerfect.

Double Indent. To move an entire paragraph in one tab stop from both the left and right margins.

Draft view. A perspective of your document that does not display certain features such as footers, headers, and watermarks that might exist in the document. Because not all features appear onscreen, working in Draft view is often faster than working in Page view.

Drag-and-drop. To move text or an object by positioning the mouse pointer on the item you want to move, pressing and holding the mouse button, dragging the mouse pointer, and then releasing the mouse button to drop the material into its new location.

Drop cap. Single letters that decorate text at the beginning of a line or paragraph.

Endnote. Reference information that prints at the end of a document.

Field. A piece of information used in a data file or a form file for the purpose of mail merge.

File. Information stored on a disk under a single name.

File format. The arrangement and organization of information in a file. File format is determined by the application that created the file.

Fill. The background color or pattern of an object such as a cell of a table or a paragraph.

Font. A group of letters, numbers, and symbols with a common typeface.

Footer. Text entered in an area of a document that will be displayed at the bottom of each page of the document.

Footnote. Reference information that prints at the bottom of the page.

Form file. A file used in the Merge process that can be made up of text, formatting, graphics, and merge codes. A form file is created just like a regular document, but instead of placing specific information in certain places, you insert a field or code that will be replaced by information from the data file when you perform the merge.

Format. To change the appearance of text or objects with features such as the font, style, color, borders, and size.

Go To. To jump to a specific page or location of your document quickly.

Grammatik. The grammar-checking feature of WordPerfect.

Gridlines. The lines dividing rows and columns in a table.

Handles. Small black squares that appear when you select an object and enable you to resize the object.

Hanging Indent. To move all but the first line of a paragraph one tab stop to the right.

Header. Text entered in an area of a document that will be displayed at the top of each page of the document.

Highlight. To put a bar of transparent color over text.

Hypertext link. A connection from the current document to another document or to a document on the World Wide Web.

Icon. A small graphic image that represents an application, command, or tool. An action is performed when an icon is clicked or double-clicked.

Indent. To move a complete paragraph one tab stop to the right.

Internet Publisher. Feature that lets you create and edit documents for the World Wide Web and launch Web browser software to browse the World Wide Web.

Justification. *See* Alignment.

Landscape. Orientation of a page in which the long edge of the paper runs horizontally.

Line Height. The distance between the top of one line of text and the top of the next line of text. Ordinarily, it is set according to the font being used.

Line Numbering. Feature that numbers the lines in a document and prints each line number.

Line Spacing. The amount of space between lines of text.

Macro. A series of commands and keystrokes stored in a file that can be replayed by a few keystrokes or a mouse click.

Mail Merge. A feature that uses data from a data file and combines it with a document called a form file to produce personalized letters.

Margin. The width of blank space from the edge of the page to the edge of the text. All four sides of a page have margins.

Mouse pointer. A symbol that indicates a position onscreen as you move the mouse around on your desk.

Open. To start an application, to insert a document into a new document window, or to access a dialog box.

Orientation. A setting that designates whether a document will print with text running along the long or short side of a piece of paper.

Page Break. A command that tells WordPerfect to begin a new page.

Page view. Displays a document the way it will look when printed. Page view displays fonts and appearance features, headers, footers, footnotes, watermarks, rotated text, and label arrangement.

Paste. To retrieve information stored on the Clipboard and insert a copy of it into a WordPerfect document.

PerfectExpert. A built-in Help program for WordPerfect that lets you ask for the Help information you need in your own words. The PerfectExpert searches through all the main Help files, and then lists topics that are the best match for your question.

Point. To move the mouse until the tip of the mouse pointer rests on an item.

Point size. A unit of measurement used to indicate font size. One point is 1/72" in height.

Portrait. The orientation of the page in which the long edge of the page runs vertically.

Print Preview. Shows you how your printed document will look onscreen before you print it.

Prompt-As-You-Go. A feature on the Property Bar that displays suggestions while you type. Prompt-As-You-Go can act as a spell checker, a grammar checker, or a thesaurus, depending on where the insertion point is placed.

Property Bar. Appears at the top of the application window and is used to access the features available in WordPerfect. Similar to a Toolbar, except the Property Bar will change according to the current task.

QuickCorrect. A feature that automatically corrects common spelling mistakes (such as "teh" for "the").

QuickFormat. A feature that enables you to easily copy formatting applied to text to any other text.

QuickLinks. A feature that automatically creates hyperlinks when you type certain kinds of text.

Redo. To reverse the last Undo action.

Reveal Codes. A feature that allows you to see the hidden markers that control how a document appears on the screen and prints.

Right-align. To line up text with the right side of a tab setting or document margin, as with a row of numbers in a column.

Ruler. A feature that lets you easily change page format elements such as tabs and margins.

Save. To take a document residing in the memory of the computer and create a file to be stored on a disk.

Scrapbook. A collection of clip art provided by WordPerfect.

Scroll bars. The bars on the right side and bottom of a window that let you move vertically and horizontally through a document.

Shadow Cursor. The icon that moves through the document as you move the mouse on your desk. This cursor shows exactly where the insertion point will go when you click the mouse. You can click anywhere to start typing text, or drag to insert clip art, a text box, or a table.

Shape. Items such as a circle, rectangle, line, polygon, or polyline in your document.

Sort. To arrange data in alphabetical or numeric order.

SpeedFormat. A feature that enables you to apply predefined sets of formatting to a table.

Spell Check. A feature that checks the spelling of words in your document against a dictionary and flags possible errors for correction.

Style. A way to format similar types of text such as headings and lists.

Suppress. To temporarily turn off a header, footer, watermark, or page number.

Symbols. Characters that are not on your keyboard, such as iconic symbols, phonetic characters, and characters in other alphabets.

Tabs. Settings in your document to determine where the insertion point moves when you press the tab key or use the indent feature.

Table. A set of rows and columns of cells that you fill in with text, numbers, or graphics.

Template. A document file with customized format, content, and features. Frequently used to create faxes, memos, and proposals.

TextArt. A feature that lets you add special effects to text, such as curving the text or making text three-dimensional.

Text box. A type of graphic box that can be used for placing and rotating text.

Thesaurus. A feature used to find synonyms (words that are alike) and antonyms (words that are opposite).

Toolbar. Set of control buttons that appears at the top of the application window and is used to access the features available in WordPerfect. Similar to a Property Bar, except it does not change according to the current task.

Undo. To reverse the last editing action.

Undo/Redo History. Feature that allows you to track and reverse up to 300 actions in your document. You can save a history of those actions with a document so you can undo or redo actions after closing the document and then opening it again.

Uppercase. A capital letter.

Views. Ways of displaying documents to see different perspectives of the information in that document.

Watermark. A background image behind the text on a page. Clip art images, an existing file, or text can be used for the watermark.

Word Wrap. To let text in a paragraph automatically flow to the next line when it reaches the right margin.

Zoom. To enlarge or reduce the way text is displayed onscreen. It does not affect how the document will print.

Index

Send Us
YOUR COMMENTS

Dear Reader:

Thank you for buying this book. In order to offer you more quality books on the topics *you* would like to see, we need your input. At Prima Publishing, we pride ourselves on timely responsiveness to our readers needs. If you'll complete and return this brief questionnaire, *we will listen!*

Name: (first) _____ (M.I.) _____ (last) _____

Company: _____ Type of business: _____

Address: _____ City: _____ State: _____ Zip: _____

Phone: _____ Fax: _____ E-mail address: _____

May we contact you for research purposes? ❏ Yes ❏ No

(If you participate in a research project, we will supply you with your choice of a book from Prima CPD)

---

1 How would you rate this book, overall?

❏ Excellent ❏ Fair
❏ Very Good ❏ Below Average
❏ Good ❏ Poor

2 Why did you buy this book?

❏ Price of book ❏ Content
❏ Author's reputation ❏ Prima's reputation
❏ CD-ROM/disk included with book
❏ Information highlighted on cover
❏ Other (Please specify): _____

3 How did you discover this book?

❏ Found it on bookstore shelf
❏ Saw it in Prima Publishing catalog
❏ Recommended by store personnel
❏ Recommended by friend or colleague
❏ Saw an advertisement in: _____
❏ Read book review in: _____
❏ Saw it on Web site: _____
❏ Other (Please specify): _____

4 Where did you buy this book?

❏ Bookstore (name)_____
❏ Computer Store (name) _____
❏ Electronics Store (name) _____
❏ Wholesale Club (name) _____
❏ Mail Order (name) _____
❏ Direct from Prima Publishing
❏ Other (please specify): _____

5 Which computer periodicals do you read regularly? _____
_____
_____

6 Would you like to see your name in print?

May we use your name and quote you in future Prima Publishing books or promotional materials?

❏ Yes ❏ No

---

7 Comments & Suggestions: _____
_____
_____

8 Where do you use your computer?

Work	❏ 100%	❏ 75%	❏ 50%	❏ 25%
Home	❏ 100%	❏ 75%	❏ 50%	❏ 25%
School	❏ 100%	❏ 75%	❏ 50%	❏ 25%

Other _____

9 How do you rate your level of computer skills?

❏ Beginner
❏ Advanced
❏ Intermediate

10 What is your age?

❏ Under 18
❏ 18-24   ❏ 40-49
❏ 25-29   ❏ 50-59
❏ 30-39   ❏ 60-over

11 I would be interested in computer books on these topics

❏ Word Processing   ❏ Database:
❏ Networking   ❏ Spreadsheets
❏ Desktop Publishing ❏ Web site design

Other _____

SAVE A STAMP

Visit our Web Site at: **http://www.primapublishing.com**
and simply fill in one of our online Response Forms

Prima's Visual Learning Guides

fast & easy

Relax, learning new software is now a breeze. You are looking at a series of books dedicated to one idea: To help you learn to use software as quickly and easily as possible. No need to wade through boring pages of endless text. With Prima's Visual Learning Guides, you simply look and learn.

ACT! 3
Dick Cravens
0-7615-1175-X
352 pgs.
$16.99 (Can. $23.95)

Word 97
Nancy Stevenson
0-7615-1007-9
384 pgs.
$16.99 (Can. $23.95)

Excel 97
Nancy Stevenson
0-7615-1008-7
352 pgs.
$16.99 (Can. $23.95)

Office 97
Elaine Marmel
0-7615-1162-8
432 pgs.
$16.99 (Can. $23.95)

Windows® 95
Grace Joely Beatty, Ph.D.
David C. Gardner, Ph.D.
1-55958-738-5
288 pgs.
$19.95 (Can. $29.95)

WordPerfect® 6.1 for Windows
Grace Joely Beatty, Ph.D.
David C. Gardner, Ph.D.
0-7615-0091-X
288 pgs.
$19.95 (Can. $29.95)

Excel 5 for Windows®
Grace Joely Beatty, Ph.D.
David C. Gardner, Ph.D.
1-55958-736-9
288 pgs.
$19.95 (Can. $29.95)

IMA

http://www.primapublishing.com

OTHER BOOKS FROM PRIMA PUBLISHING
Computer Products Division

ISBN	Title	Price	Release Date
0-7615-1175-X	Act! 3 Visual Learning Guide	$16.99	Summer '97
0-7615-0680-2	America Online Complete Handbook and Membership Kit	$24.99	Available Now
0-7615-0417-6	CompuServe Complete Handbook and Membership Kit	$24.95	Available Now
0-7615-0692-6	Create Your First Web Page in a Weekend	$29.99	Available Now
0-7615-0743-4	Create FrontPage Web Pages in a Weekend	$29.99	Available Now
0-7615-0428-1	The Essential Excel 97 Book	$27.99	Available Now
0-7615-0733-7	The Essential Netscape Communicator Book	$24.99	Summer '97
0-7615-0969-0	The Essential Office 97 Book	$27.99	Available Now
0-7615-0695-0	The Essential Photoshop Book	$35.00	Available Now
0-7615-1182-2	The Essential PowerPoint 97 Book	$24.99	Available Now
0-7615-1136-9	The Essential Publisher 97 Book	$24.99	Available Now
0-7615-0752-3	The Essential Windows NT 4 Book	$27.99	Available Now
0-7615-0427-3	The Essential Word 97 Book	$27.99	Available Now
0-7615-0425-7	The Essential WordPerfect 8 Book	$24.99	Summer '97
0-7615-1008-7	Excel 97 Visual Learning Guide	$16.99	Available Now
0-7615-1193-8	Lotus 1-2-3 97 Visual Learning Guide	$16.99	Summer '97

ISBN	Title	Price	Release Date
0-7615-0852-X	Netscape Navigator 3 Complete Handbook	$24.99	Available Now
0-7615-1162-8	Office 97 Visual Learning Guide	$16.99	Available Now
0-7615-0759-0	Professional Web Design	$40.00	Available Now
0-7615-0063-4	Researching on the Internet	$29.95	Available Now
0-7615-0686-1	Researching on the World Wide Web	$24.99	Available Now
0-7615-1192-X	SmartSuite 97 Visual Learning Guide	$16.99	Summer '97
0-7615-1007-9	Word 97 Visual Learning Guide	$16.99	Available Now
0-7615-1188-1	WordPerfect Suite 8 Visual Learning Guide	$16.99	Summer '97

TO ORDER BOOKS

Please send me the following items:

Quantity	Title	Unit Price	Total
_____	_____	$_____	$_____
_____	_____	$_____	$_____
_____	_____	$_____	$_____
_____	_____	$_____	$_____
_____	_____	$_____	$_____

Subtotal	$_____
Deduct 10% when ordering 3–5 books	$_____
7.25% Sales Tax (CA only)	$_____
8.25% Sales Tax (TN only)	$_____
5.0% Sales Tax (MD and IN only)	$_____
Shipping and Handling*	$_____
TOTAL ORDER	$_____

Shipping and Handling depend on Subtotal.

Subtotal	Shipping/Handling
$0.00–$14.99	$3.00
$15.00–29.99	$4.00
$30.00–49.99	$6.00
$50.00–99.99	$10.00
$100.00–199.99	$13.00
$200.00+	call for quote

Foreign and all Priority Request orders:
Call Order Entry department for price quote
at 1-916-632-4400

This chart represents the total retail price of books
only (before applicable discounts are taken).

By telephone: With Visa or MC, call 1-800-632-8676. Mon.–Fri. 8:30–4:00 PST.

By Internet e-mail: sales@primapub.com

By mail: Just fill out the information below and send with your remittance to:

PRIMA PUBLISHING

P.O. Box 1260BK

Rocklin, CA 95677-1260

http://www.primapublishing.com

Name_____ Daytime Telephone_____

Address _____

City _____ State _____ Zip_____

Visa /MC# _____Exp. _____

Check/Money Order enclosed for $_____ Payable to Prima Publishing

Signature_____